William Butler Yeats

ESSAYS IN TRIBUTE

Edited by

STEPHEN GWYNN

KENNIKAT PRESS
Port Washington, New York
1965

WILLIAM BUTLER YEATS

Published in 1940 under title "Scattering Branches"
Reissued in 1965 by Kennikat Press
Manufactured in U.S.A. by Arno Press, Inc.

Library of Congress Catalog Card No: 65-20466

PREFACE

THREE NAMES ARE MISSING FROM THIS ASSEMBLY which I desired to include. But the Poet Laureate had already spoken his brief emphatic tribute in *The Arrow* and did not, in this tragic time, feel able to do more. T. S. Eliot preferred to write at his own leisure and to his own limit. Oliver Gogarty was fully occupied in a lecture tour through the United States.

But these three poets may be counted as fully with the rest of us in paying homage.

S. G.

May 1940

CONTENTS

Contents

I

SCATTERING BRANCHES

BY STEPHEN GWYNN

When the Trojan maiden, Polyxena, died valiantly, the Greek host by whom she was sacrificed, vying with one another in respect to the dead, scattered on her what leaves and branches they could find. When an Irish poet had lived valiantly, it was only right that some such tribute should be paid, above all by those of his own allegiance.

Yeats had a double capacity : the servant of his art and the servant of Ireland. Tribute was paid at once, and fittingly, in a publication, *The Arrow*, which on far separated occasions has been launched from the institution whose mainstay he was — the Irish national theatre. It was thought well, however, that something should be done to put the same homage in a less fugitive expression of what was felt at his death in the general world of art and letters.

When I was asked to bring together such a

group of contributions as will be found here, my only justification for accepting was that I had known him longer perhaps than any other living man of letters, longer even than the closest of all his comrades, the one to whom he owed most. While he was still an art student, I was an undergraduate, seeing much of the group which he frequented in Dublin. Professor Dowden's house was a place where they often met, and most of them were several years older than Yeats ; more than one, such as Rolleston and J. F. Taylor, had already begun to establish a reputation. Men of five-and-twenty or thirty do not often think an untidy lad more important than themselves ; but it is a fact that all of them regarded Yeats, before he had published a line, as the poet who was to give to Ireland what Ireland in their judgment most needed. For we were all painfully conscious that Ireland then had little to show in the field of literature ; we were in particular envious of Scotland's prestige. Things are changed now. Far be it from me to say that Yeats did for Ireland what Burns or even Walter Scott did for their country ; but on the last fifty years Ireland can make a showing in literature that may face any reasonable comparison without discredit. That change in the balance Yeats accomplished, directly by his own work and indirectly by his example and influence.

What Scott and Burns achieved by their popularity, Yeats had to achieve without it. He was never able to command a ready audience in Ireland, and his countrymen knew him first as an arrogant young man, telling them that what they had counted magnificent poetry was at best mediocre, and at worst cheap rhetoric. He succeeded through the few, and is a notable example of what can be done by disregarding the many.

For a long time, I admired, apart from the quality of his poetry, chiefly his courage. But now, looking back over the whole, it is the dignity of his life that I would praise. He was a dedicated person, like Milton, self-appointed, and except in Milton, I can recall no other example of such long and renewing growth. Other poets, Tennyson and Browning, to name the nearest, have written and written well over as long a period ; but with them we get only a mellowing of the same fruit. With Yeats as with Milton, we find the same tree yielding something so different in quality that it is almost new in kind. I am not asking that Yeats should be set on a level with Milton, but there is a real analogy. Technically, each of them carried the art of writing in verse to a perfection unsurpassed in his own day ; each of them converted to the purposes of his art all the experiences of his life ; each was indefatigable in the pursuit of his art ; but neither of them took the easy way of saying that the pursuit of art absolved him from answering other calls which might seem an interruption.

It is not an easy matter for a man without money to be a poet and only a poet. Even with his great gifts, Yeats achieved it by learning to do without money. If he ever wrote anything simply for the money it would bring in, it was in the early days when body and soul had to be kept together ; but after he had made a name among the small public which is interested in poetry, it would have been easy to turn this reputation into cash by writing for periodicals which would have liked to include him among their contributors ; and he never did so. The stronger his position, the more determined he was to write only what he desired to write ; and so he dispensed with much that he could have gained without the least discredit. In short, he lived an ascetic life — continuously an athlete.

In one thing he must be counted fortunate — though indeed this was no casual bounty of Providence but a profound expression of his nature. Yet lucky he was that in youth he should meet a woman of his own age, of extraordinary beauty, and of a nobleness to match it. It did not make his life easy that she was a born revolutionary, not disposed to sit down, contented and giving content, by any hearth. It may be she never gave him happiness ; but she gave enchantment and the closest companionship ; witness his own testimony, in a complaint of sudden change in her ; the melancholy does not hide the gratitude.

> All through the years of our youth
> Neither could have known

> Their own thought from the other's,
> We were so much at one.

She gave inspiration, long after her presence was withdrawn from his life ; the passages about the memory of that intimacy are even finer than those manifestly written to be laid at her feet.

Such a passion is the best thing in the world to keep a man strenuous, and clear of all fatty degeneration of the heart.

I think also that she prevented him from becoming lost in a vague mysticism ; and, in binding him to the service of Ireland, — because it was her service also, — she helped to make humanity real to him, as it never seemed to be real and vital to the lad that I remember, — preoccupied solely with himself. He certainly never learnt to love the Irish people, but he learnt, as Swift did, to be aware of their needs. Where Swift saw miserable poverty, Yeats saw intellectual starvation ; and it was a purpose growing through his life to nourish the mind of Ireland. In pursuit of that purpose, he developed not only a talent for leadership ; he proved him-self, what nobody would have guessed in his youth, admirably gifted for co-operation, and for finding men and women that he could work with. The first attempt with Moore and Edward Martyn was a failure ; both these men were endeavouring to use the existing English stage ; but when Yeats saw the group of ardent amateurs whom W. G. Fay had assembled, he seems to have realised at once that here was the makings of a companionship, free of the conventional tradition. Fay's paper in this volume makes it clear that they all went to school together ; it indicates that here also Maud Gonne was once more a connecting link between the poet and the Irish people. But it naturally does not say, what is the truth, that Yeats had come on an actor of genius, and of an original mind. Lady Gregory assisted from the first, and was invaluable ; but Fay was essential. Among the three of them, they discovered Synge ; yet before Synge had contributed anything, they were able to impress profoundly a London audience which included such critics as Archer and Walkley. But at their second visit to London, when they were seen in a regular theatre, Synge's plays were the main feature ; *Riders to the Sea* and *The Shadow of the Glen* stood out, as *The Hour-Glass* and *Cathleen ni Houlihan* had stood out when they played a year earlier in the little hall at Queen's Gate. Jealousy had made trouble in the relations with Moore and Martyn ; it never entered between Synge and Yeats. In truth Yeats fought for Synge's work as perhaps he might have been too disdainful to fight for anything of his own.

When the trouble arose about *The Playboy*, things had at last after lean years begun to go better for the Abbey Theatre ; Boyle's comedies had brought in an element of popular satire, easily understood and appreciated ; now, the whole of this public acceptance was jeopardised. Persons of importance — (John Dillon, for instance) — came to Yeats and said, " We like your work, we like Lady Gregory's, we like Colum's ; why sacrifice all you have gained for the sake of an eccentric talent ? " But Yeats persisted, and as everybody knows, he won. Within a year *The Playboy* was being performed under normal conditions in the same house, and Synge till his death was a chief glory of the

Abbey Theatre.   In his plays a succession of
admirable actors and actresses made their reputation.

Under the joint inspiration of Yeats, Synge
and Lady Gregory, but always with Yeats as the
dominant influence — the Abbey became, it is
generally agreed, a most remarkable school of
acting.   The Fays, I think, were the chief agents
in transmitting that inspiration and translating
it into their own art ; but as an enterprise, the
theatre was successfully and continuously conducted by poets.   I do not know of any other
in which the writer has had so predominant a
part ; and assuredly the art of the actors has
not suffered by that predominance.   More than
literary excellence was needed to bring about such
a result, and its achievement is a testimony to
the force of personality that was in Yeats, and
to his masterful ability.

Everything that he did or said bore his distinctive impress.   In public speaking he had
an eloquence, which I cannot call unsurpassed,
though I am sure I never heard any one more
eloquent, because it was different in kind from

the manner and the matter of other speakers. His literary judgment was personal almost to narrowness ; he had no use for the simplicities of poetry ; and the older he grew the more he inclined to the abstract, the intellectual. In the *Oxford Book of Modern Verse* which he edited, the selection from his own work omits nearly all the things by which I believe he will be most intimately remembered — those in which *la passion parle toute pure.*

I like best myself the work of his middle period, though with a great affection for his early experiments in ballad form, " the old priest Peter Gilligan ", and the dying foxhunter. Yet he never wrote better, nor with a finer dignity, than in *A Prayer for my Daughter*, out of which there is thrown, with angry vehemence, a backward glance on the always present memory of what he had loved so long.

Of his later work in general, I am no proper judge ; accents unfamiliar to me had come into poetry, and I, who never learnt to accustom myself to them, must admire the suppleness with which Yeats adapted himself to the new ;

influenced by it, accepting it, giving and taking to the last. He was for five-and-fifty years a poet of his own time ; too constantly alert in the study of his art ever to be outmoded ; never too old to be learner as well as teacher ; never content to be always gathering the same laurels.

Some of the younger men in his own craft say here what they thought of him, how they felt towards him. Of those outside it, I know one significant instance which tells how he was regarded. After the Irish Free State came into being, its first Senate was in part filled by nomination, and Mr. Cosgrave, then President, appointed Yeats amongst others. The new state, born of a revolution, was born facing a civil war ; after it, the army brought together for that purpose did not easily settle down. There were ugly signs of disaffection, and some of the prominent officers wished to convey a warning unofficially. It was to Yeats that they chose to come, putting the matter in his hands. He, after consultation with a friend, went to Kevin O'Higgins, as in his judgment the strongest man in that Government, and found him already preparing to deal with the trouble. This is not to suggest that Yeats played an important part in resolving that crisis ; but when I learnt the facts — after Yeats was dead — it appeared to me extraordinarily significant that young men, after full experience of rebellion and of civil war, should have turned at that moment to a poet. It showed their estimate of his character and of his standing in the state.

I do not attempt any general summing up. That is done at the end by Strong, as I think with authority, and since his work is of England, no less than of Ireland, it is done without local partiality. The order in which the other contributions are placed has been arrived at after much hesitation. Only one thing was clear : the first words should be spoken by the one who was closest to his youth. But after all, the order does not matter ; each man brings his branch ; I throw down mine, and make way.

II
YEATS AND IRELAND

BY MAUD GONNE

" Nor may I less be counted one
  With Davis, Mangan, Ferguson,
  Because to him who ponders well
  My rhymes more than their rhyming tell."

" But we have hidden in our hearts the flame out of the eyes
  Of Cathleen, the daughter of Houlihan."

Yᴇᴀᴛs's ᴏᴡɴ ʟɪɴᴇs ᴛᴇʟʟ Yᴇᴀᴛs's sᴛᴏʀʏ better than any can write it — and his story is part of Ireland's story.

A tall lanky boy with deep-set dark eyes behind glasses, over which a lock of dark hair was constantly falling, to be pushed back impatiently by long sensitive fingers, often stained with paint — dressed in shabby clothes that none noticed (except himself, as he confessed long after) — a tall girl with masses of gold-brown hair and a beauty which made her Paris clothes equally unnoticeable, sat figuratively and sometimes literally, at the feet of a thin elderly man, with eagle eyes, whose unbroken will had turned the outrage of long convict imprisonment into immense dignity. He never spoke of that imprisonment. . . . John O'Leary, the master, and his two favourite disciples, William Butler Yeats and Maud Gonne.

O'Leary was the symbol of the Fenian faith, he was not a revolutionary leader. Theoretically he would have freed Ireland by the sword — and he objected to dynamite ! Because of his nobleness, he had many disciples, but these two, I think, ranked highest in his affection, and on them he set high hopes. In his little room in Temple Street they sat surrounded by books, books on shelves and books in piles on chairs and on the floor ; and Willie Yeats said there must be more books, — new books for a new generation. The master told him to leave the Art School and write them.

O'Leary's disciples organised meetings to promote book clubs and literary societies, at which O'Leary presided and Maud Gonne and Willie Yeats spoke. After the meetings the master criticised the oratory, for though he himself was no orator and not much of a writer, he was an admirable critic of style. He was more indulgent to me than to Willie ; I, having studied for the stage, in those days had better diction, and though very proud of the praise I felt it was unfair, for Willie's speeches were more

sincere than mine ; I was always concealing the
foolishness of a thought which kept intruding
on my mind — how few had ever read those
dusty volumes on the shelves, on the chairs and
on the floor. Being young and hasty, I secretly
felt action not books was needed ; I did not
then realise how the written word may lead to
action and I drifted off to speak at other
meetings held on wild hillsides, where resistance
to evictions was being organised.

Agrarianism and Parliamentarianism were
taboo to O'Leary's group of the Irish Republican
Brotherhood, and I incurred the sad displeasure
of the master and was only pardoned after the
persistent and generous intercession of my fellow
pupil Willie Yeats, who by this time had
renounced painting for writing and presented
me with a specially bound copy of his first book,
Dhoya, illustrated by A.E., then a shaggy-haired
accountant, attending night classes in the Art
School.

During long walks in the Dublin mountains,
Willie told me of his plans for a great literary
movement for the glory of Ireland, and recited

many poems he had written.

We were both held by the mysterious power of the land.   To me Ireland was the all-protecting mother, who had to be released from the bondage of the foreigner, to be free and able to protect her children ; to Willie, less aware of the People than of the Land, Ireland was the beauty of unattainable perfection, and he had to strive to express that beauty so that all should worship. His song of Red Hanrahan expresses this :

The old brown thorn-trees break in two high over
        Cummen Strand,
Under a bitter black wind that blows from the left
        hand ;
Our courage breaks like an old tree in a black wind and
        dies,
But we have hidden in our hearts the flame out of the
        eyes
Of Cathleen, the daughter of Houlihan.

The wind has bundled up the clouds high over Knocknarea,
And thrown the thunder on the stones for all that
        Maeve can say.
Angers that are like noisy clouds have set our hearts
        abeat ;

But we have all bent low and low and kissed the quiet
    feet
Of Cathleen, the daughter of Houlihan.

The yellow pool has overflowed high up on Clooth-
    na-Bare,
For the wet winds are blowing out of the clinging air ;
Like heavy flooded waters our bodies and our blood ;
But purer than a tall candle before the Holy Rood
Is Cathleen, the daughter of Houlihan.

Willie describes his own ambition and our
belief in the unifying power of the land in his
book *Four Years* (1887–1891), written in 1921,
though it only faintly shows the joyous exhilara-
tion and strength this belief gave us in the days
when we climbed so easily Croagh Patrick and
the Golden Spear mountain.

Might I not, with health and good luck to aid me,
create some new " Prometheus Unbound ", Patrick or
Columcille, Oisin or Fionn, in Prometheus's stead,
and instead of Caucasus, Croagh Patrick or Ben
Bulben ? Have not all races had their first unity from
a polytheism that marries them to rock and hill ?
We had in Ireland imaginative stories, which the
uneducated classes knew and even sang, and might we
not make these stories current among the educated

classes, rediscovering for the work's sake, what I have called " the applied arts of literature " the association of literature, that is, with music, speech and dance ? and at last, it might be, so deepen the political passion of the nation, that all, artist and poet, craftsman and day labourer would accept a common design ?

Perhaps even these images, once created and associated with river and mountain, might move themselves, and with some powerful, even turbulent, life ! . . .

Much of his childhood had been spent amid the weird and tragic loveliness of Sligo's mountains and the mystery of its lakes ; from this western magic, even in London where circumstances led him, he never escaped ; it was part of him and turned his mind to mystic thought and to beauty heart-rending in its intensity.

The land of Ireland, we both felt, was powerfully alive and invisibly peopled, and whenever we grew despondent over the weakness of the national movement, we went to it for comfort. If only we could make contact with the hidden forces of the land it would give us strength for the freeing of Ireland. Most of our talk centred round this and it led us both into strange places, from which I, less daring in thought, if more daring in action, than Willie, drew back, lest it might lead me away and not into the heart of Ireland's hidden strength.

One of our early dreams was a Castle of the Heroes. It was to be in the middle of a lake, a shrine of Irish tradition where only those who had dedicated their lives to Ireland might penetrate ; they were to be brought there in a painted boat across the lake and might only stay for short periods of rest and inspiration. It was to be built of Irish stone and decorated only with the Four Jewels of the Tuatha de Danaan, with perhaps a statue of Ireland, if any artist could be found great enough to make one, which we doubted.

The Four Jewels, as Willie explained, are universal symbols appearing in debased form on the Tarot, the divining cards of the Egyptians and even on our own playing cards, and foreshadowed the Christian symbolism of the Saint Grail, whose legends Willie loved to trace to Ireland.

The Lia Fail, the Stone of Destiny, he said, corresponded with the Altar, which, as Catholics know, even when made of wood should have a stone embedded in it ;

The Cauldron of the Dagda, the Good God, called also the Cauldron of Recompense, the Chalice, the Grail Cup ;

The Golden Spear of Victory of Lugh the Sun God, the Lance which pierced the side of Christ for the salvation of mankind ;

The Sword of Light, the Cross-handled sword of the Crusaders, or the Knights of the Grail.

Willie loved symbols, to crystallise his thoughts, and he meditated much on them. All trivialities were to be excluded from the Castle of the Heroes ; only things combining beauty with utility were to be admitted in its furnishing. In austere comfort those setting forth on some great task for Ireland might through lonely meditation on Ireland harmonise their individual effort with national endeavour.

Our Castle of the Heroes remained a Castle

in the Air, but the last time I saw Willie at Riversdale just before he left Ireland for the last time, as we said goodbye, he, sitting in his arm-chair from which he could rise only with great effort, said, " Maud, we should have gone on with our Castle of the Heroes, we might still do it ". I was so surprised that he remembered, I could not reply. The whirlpool of life had sent the current of our activities wide apart. We had quarrelled seriously when he became a Senator of the Free State which voted Flogging Acts against young republican soldiers still seek-ing to free Ireland from the contamination of the British Empire, and for several years we had ceased to meet. I stood speechless beside him with the song of Red Hanrahan echoing through my mind, " Angers that are like noisy clouds have set our hearts abeat " — " Like heavy flooded waters our bodies and our blood ", and I realised that Willie and I still " bent low and low and kissed the quiet feet " and worshipped Her, who is " purer than a tall candle before the Holy Rood ".

He is gone, and I am a prisoner of old age

waiting for release. The Ireland I live in is very different from the Ireland of our dreams, because our dream is not yet achieved ; the quiet island on the lake over which heroes were to row in a painted boat, has no Castle of simple magnificence built to shelter them momentarily from the " bitter black wind " of confusion " which blows from the left hand " though perhaps some behind prison bars may build one deep in their own hearts.

Looking out from my own prison-house I can see the great work for Ireland accomplished by my fellow pupil of long ago.

What if Yeats wrote in a language which is not the language of Ireland that the English worked hard to obliterate ? Spirits need no language to transmit their thought, and the Spirit of Ireland spoke through Willie Yeats, telling of unspeakable beauty and of its heroic call. Nations like men are created in God's image, the image of the most Blessed Trinity — the People, the Land and, from their love proceeding, the Spirit of Life, its creative force which alone can make Nations separate entities.

In each generation that Spirit chooses its instrument of expression from among the people, and when it speaks through them, their words and acts have extraordinary significance and extraordinary power.

Without Yeats there would have been no Literary Revival in Ireland. Without the inspiration of that Revival and the glorification of beauty and heroic virtue, I doubt if there would have been an Easter Week. They were poets and writers who led Irish youth to die, that Ireland might live ; and because of them and their writings, when they were crushed by the brute force of England, the people did not yield as they did after the crushing of the Fenian rising. In 1918 by heroic effort Ireland triumphed over overwhelming force and, filled with spiritual exultation, the people accomplished miracles.

Yeats's aloofness and his intolerance of mediocrity, a spiritual pride which is dangerous, tended to keep him apart from the first person of the National Trinity, the People. He hated crowds, I loved them. His generous desire to help and share my work brought him into contact with crowds and with all sorts of people, men from the country and men from the towns, working for Ireland's freedom. I hardly realised then how important that contact was to him and sometimes felt guilty at taking so much of his time from his literary work. As we sat together through the boredom of conventions and long committee meetings, where his dominating personality and practical grasp of detail made him a powerful ally, it sometimes seemed like using a fine Toledo blade instead of a loy in the spade-work of political organisation ; but I remember Willie's astonished pleasure when, after a meeting, some shy boy would come up and shake his hand because he had read his poems and loved them ; I know that contact was good for him. After my marriage and during my long sojourn in France, he lost this contact and became more unaware of the forces working for Ireland's freedom. His search for hidden knowledge had led him so far along strange paths that he at times almost forgot the object of the quest. He found himself among the comfortable and well-fed, who style themselves the " upper classes ", but whom Willie, shuddering at the words and discriminating even among them, called " Distinguished Persons " ; and some of them undoubtedly deserved the title. Willie's own absorption in Ireland and his strong personality succeeded in awakening in some of them the desire to work for Ireland ; but the attitude of the well-fed is often patronising to the Shan Van Vocht, not reverent.

The Abbey and its peasant plays catered for their amusement ; but Willie's own plays were seldom performed there because he could not write down to their level, and concealed the fact from himself by saying that the actors could not act up to his ; they couldn't speak his verse. There was a time when he would have taught them to, for he was a marvellous teacher, and if the first performance of his *Cathleen ni Houlihan* has been unequalled since, it is because Willie himself worked at those rehearsals and taught the boys and girls who could only come to rehearsals on Sundays, or in the evenings, when released from workshops and shop counters, the exact expression he wanted for his words. The effect of that play on the crowd which nightly filled the little hall in Clarendon Street was such that after the first week, powerful intervention was used to evict us from it and so stop the performance. In those days he was very reverent to the Shan Van Vocht and to her children and would not allow any to be patronising towards her. He was a patient teacher, though I can imagine him impatient, for he never suffered fools gladly ; but his anger could only be really aroused by attacks on any one he looked on as his own, or at any slight, real or imaginary, on the few he called his friends. Attack on himself he did not resent.

Willie had always desired a Theatre of our own and his determination to have one was strengthened by the incident of our eviction from our hall during the first production of *Cathleen ni Houlihan*. It required money, and Willie got the money from those not interested in Ireland's freedom, and this led up to our first quarrel, but that is too long a story to be told here and it is not important because it was not a serious quarrel.

After O'Leary died, Willie wrote :

> Romantic Ireland's dead and gone,
> It's with O'Leary in the grave.

He wrote this because he had lost contact with those who were working for Ireland's freedom. So in 1916, before the magnificent flowering of the seed he had sown with pious exaltation, but left others to water, he stood amazed and abashed. In this mood he came to me in France where I was marooned by the World War. I found his mood hard to understand. The struggle of his mind can be read in his poem on Easter 1916, with its refrain :

> All changed, changed utterly :
> A terrible beauty is born.
>
> .   .   .   .
>
> Hearts with one purpose alone
> Through summer and winter seem
> Enchanted to a stone
> To trouble the living stream.
>
> .   .   .   .
>
> Too long a sacrifice
> Can make a stone of the heart.

Standing by the seashore in Normandy in September 1916 he read me that poem; he had worked on it all the night before, and he implored me to forget the stone and its inner fire for the flashing, changing joy of life ; but when he found my mind dull with the stone of the fixed idea of getting back to Ireland, kind and helpful as ever, he helped me to overcome political and passport difficulties and we travelled as far as London together. In London we parted ; my road led to jail with Constance de Markievicz, and Cathleen Clarke, but Willie's road was more difficult, a road of outer peace and inner confusion, discernible in his later work. He was too old to cut a way for himself and for Ireland out of the confusion which, after the imposed Treaty of 1921, spread like a wizard's mist over the country, obscuring both the stone and the glory and joy of changing life. The Spirit of Ireland needs young instruments for its expression, it cannot speak through those whose minds are clogged by the trivialities of living and human responsibilities : Willie Yeats, like myself, had passed the allotted span of human activities.

The Sligo mountains that first revealed to him the vision of eternal beauty now claim the dead body of their son, to rest beside the cairn of Maeve among their weird grandeur.

He brought great gifts and laid them at the quiet feet of Ireland, gifts of glory which brought fame to her and to himself, for Ireland is a great giver of rewards. Those through whom the spirit has once spoken are immortal and " shall be remembered forever ", and of these is Willie Yeats.

III
YEATS AS A PAINTER SAW HIM

BY SIR WILLIAM ROTHENSTEIN

It was during 1893 that Frederick York Powell, then Regius Professor of History at Oxford, took me to the Yeats's house in Bedford Park. I found old Mr. Yeats to be in close sympathy with the Preraphaelites, but without the prejudices noticeable among the devout; he was a warm admirer of Whistler and the French Impressionists and welcomed me as an enthusiast for French painting. I do not recollect whether W. B. Yeats was then living at Bedford Park or had already taken rooms at Woburn Buildings. It was at Woburn Buildings that I saw him thenceforward.

Yeats was then lank of figure and pale, with glistening white forehead over which a black lock fell; he had long pale hands and was dressed always in dark clothes, and wore the broad, loose-flowing black tie affected by French artists and writers.

While I frequented writers as much as painters, I had little respect for their opinions on art ; yet did not fear to express, with the arrogance of youth, emphatic opinions on literature ; opinions received, perhaps because of my relations with poets and writers in Paris, with a certain indulgence. Painters, since language is common to all, have usually a broader outlook on literature than writers have on painting. Indeed, I never expect the critical eye from any but painters, while I have always enjoyed the subtle comments of poets, not on poetry alone, but on many aspects of life.

Yeats was not in fact sensitive to form or to colour. He was too easily impressed by work which showed a superficial appearance of romance or mysticism. The drawings of Blake and Rossetti, of Beardsley and Ricketts certainly appealed to him, and from Ricketts and his father he learnt much. But it was the inventive quality of his talk that appealed to me, rather than his views on the arts. For Yeats, like other Irishmen, in his talk, was the supreme artist.

I remember going one day to see George

Moore, who greeted me with, " I am so glad you have come. I can only think when I am talking !" Yeats could also think in solitude, but ideas, when he was in the mood for talking, seldom failed him. He liked women to be among his audience. A man is at his best talking to women, he said once. So at Woburn Buildings there was usually a circle of green-clad ladies seated on the floor, while he intoned his poems, and Florence Farr plucked at the single string of a rough, primitive instrument, designed by Yeats himself. In those days he was absorbed by spiritualism, and by magic too, affecting to believe in the power of certain words to evoke spirits. He hinted that he had got into communion with dark forces, and told of drawing a circle, from within which he called up spirits, spirits he believed to be on the point of materialising. He told too of an uneducated girl who, going into a trance, spoke literary Chinese. I wondered how Yeats could identify the language ! It was his disdain for science that drove him, as it drove Chesterton, into a belief in the miraculous. Since what men call reality is but an illusion, what appears to us miraculous may therefore be truer than that to which we respond through our fallible senses of sight, hearing and touch. Hence his respect for the secret knowledge, formerly handed down from generation to generation by the initiated, now forever lost. Santayana holds religion, with its symbols and dogmas, to be a form of poetry. No less so is folklore ; hence Yeats encouraged old men and women to tell him stories of fairies, of strange folk they had met, and on their experiences he built his own. His belief in the miraculous was an emotional rather than an intellectual process. For in Yeats there was a solid kernel of wisdom, a shrewd judgment of men, and of the material side of life ; he was well aware of the value of an aloofness and mystery, which he cultivated.

Robert Bridges had written to me, in 1898 : " Yeats I know. He has been here, and we want him here again — he is a true poet, and delightful company, but he is in great danger of fooling himself with Rosicrucianism and folk-lore and erotical spiritualism — some of his work is of the very best, both poetry and prose."

Already in his schooldays, the fact that his father was an artist gave him a feeling of apartness from his fellows, and his father's early sympathy with the Preraphaelites, with William Morris and William de Morgan, had its effect on the family.

In early youth we are readily drawn towards those who share our admirations ; but there was something I missed in Yeats — he had no eye. Later, when he would walk with me in the country, he seemed to notice nothing of the beauty about him ; he seemed to keep his eyes on the ground.

I made many drawings of Yeats during the late 'nineties, one especially, a lithograph published in a small series, the *Liber Juniorum*, has been frequently reproduced. Later, in 1908, Augustus John made an etching of him. Yeats didn't like it, though it was both an excellent portrait and a fine work of art.

I would like to show you Augustus John's portrait of me. A beautiful etching, and I understand what he means in it, and admire the meaning, but it is useless for my purpose. Robert Gregory agrees in this and has recommended me to show it to you.

I did my best to persuade Yeats that the etching was a masterpiece ; and Hugh Lane helped him to appreciate John's genius. In his later years he was delighted with a painting John made from him, while they were both staying with Gogarty in Connemara.

Yeats wanted me to help him to push Lane's plans for his gallery of modern art in Dublin :

Lane has asked me to try and get some people to write up the opening of his Gallery which is at 4 o'clock on January 20th, and I would like your advice. . . . It is very important to get enough notice taken of the opening of the Gallery to make the Corporation believe in Lane, for if they do, they will leave him free, and if they don't, they will sooner or later upset him in the interest of some bad patriotic painter. He has so many enemies in Dublin, that all the help we can get from outside is necessary. I wish there were any chance of you yourself coming over.

Lane's projects for a gallery of modern art in Dublin, and his hopes for a school of purely Irish painting, were on all fours with Yeats's own aims for a revival of Irish literature and drama, a revival which was in fact in great measure due to Yeats's vision and leadership.

I still remember the enthusiasm with which I saw the Irish players when they first came to London and the profound impression Synge's plays made upon me. I happened to be in New York when the Abbey company visited the States in 1911. They came to see me in my studio there, when I invited them to supper after their first night, a plan which Lady Gregory vetoed, to my disappointment, and, they said, to theirs too. While Yeats was occupied with the Theatre, he came under the influence of Gordon Craig, whose simple and majestic screens for the stage at once attracted him. From Craig's dramatic sense he learned much, though he remarked, with some wry amusement, that Craig's seemingly simple screens proved more costly than the professional scene-painter's work. Yeats was to preside at a complimentary dinner to Craig, but his disinclination to propose the King's health stood in the way, and I had to take his place in the chair.

It was soon after my return from America in

the spring of 1912 that Rabindranath Tagore came to London. I had first met Rabindranath at the Tagore family-house in Calcutta. No one then told me that he was an eminent poet and writer, but I was struck by the dignity of his person as he sat, clothed in white *chaddar* and *dhoti*, silent but attentive.

On my return to England, I read, in the *Modern Review*, a Calcutta monthly, a short story signed by Rabindranath. Soon after there came to me, from one of his schoolmasters, some rough translations of a few of his poems. I thought these strangely beautiful, and they dealt with an unfamiliar subject matter. I wanted a more reliable opinion of their quality from others, and sent copies to Andrew Bradley and to Yeats. Bradley replied at once ; it looked, he wrote, as though a new star had appeared in our firmament. From Yeats came no response. I pressed him again. Whether he had lost or mislaid the typescript I do not remember, but when he came to London from Dublin and got into touch with me he carried off the translations. There was no question of indifference. He could not sufficiently praise the poems.

Tagore, disclaiming intimate knowledge of the English tongue, had asked me to suggest improvements in his verses. Such a task was not for me. Now Yeats took up the poems, going through them line by line with Rabindranath, suggesting small changes here and there, but he was careful not to change the substance, sense or rhythm. The India Society, to whom I proposed the publication of the poems, agreed on condition that Yeats provided an introduction. About this preface Yeats wrote :

I think I had better send it to you. You will, I think, find it emphatic enough. If you like it you can say. so to Tagore. In the first little chapter I have given what Indians have said to me about Tagore — their praise of him and their description of his life. That I am anxious about — some fact may be given wrongly, and yet I don't want anything crossed out by Tagore's modesty. Every essay is an impression ; I give no facts except those in the quoted conversation.

Under the title of *Gitanjali*, a limited edition of the poems was brought out by the India

Society. *Gitanjali* brought to Rabindranath European fame, and the award of the Nobel Prize. It was said in India that the poems owed much of their success to Yeats. This was untrue ; Yeats's changes were of the slightest.

Later Tagore wrote to me of " the delightful days when I worked with Yeats and I am sure the magic of his pen helped my English to attain some quality of permanence. . . . Please thank Yeats once again on my behalf for the help which he rendered to my poems in their perilous adventure of a foreign reincarnation and assure him that I at least never under-rate the value of his literary comradeship."

The friendship between the two poets proved an enduring one ; they had much in common, both spiritually and politically. India indeed learned much of her revolutionary doctrine and example from Southern Ireland.

Yeats happened to be staying with us in Gloucestershire during the Easter of 1916 and I recollect his grave face when he read of the outbreak of the Easter rebellion. He spoke of the leaders as innocent and patriotic theorists, carried away by their belief that they must put their theories into practice. They would fail and pay the penalty for their rashness. He did not then realise how significant the sacrifice was to be for Ireland's future. He obviously felt some discomfort at being safe in England when his friends were risking their lives in Dublin, and fretted somewhat that he had not been consulted, had been left in ignorance of what was afoot.

His heart was in Ireland, yet he had spent the greater part of his life in London. Scornful of certain elements in the English character, he none the less admired the aristocratic quality of English culture ; and his relations with English poets, with Dowson, Bridges, Masefield, Binyon, Symons and Sturge Moore, were of the closest. On this account, no doubt, and because he was regarded as the most eminent contemporary poet and man of letters, he was asked to edit the *Oxford Book of Modern Verse*. While he was in London in connection with this work, I went more than once to see him in his lodgings. On one occasion I found him surrounded with a pile of books, when he asked me, did I know anything of Dorothy Wellesley's verses ? He had only lately come upon her poems and was inclined to place her high among contemporary poets. Pleased at his praise, I wrote to tell Lady Gerald of Yeats's opinion. I heard from her soon after ; (I think Lady Ottoline Morell had also spoken of Yeats's praise) Yeats was coming to stay ; would I join them at Penns in the Rocks, her Sussex home ? This was the beginning of a friendship which was to endure until Yeats's death. His first opinion of the quality of Dorothy's poems was strengthened by further reading and he now proposed to edit a selection of her verses. For this he wrote an introduction, and in due course the volume appeared, with a drawing I had made of Lady Gerald some years earlier.

I stayed more than once, with Yeats as a fellow guest, at Penns ; other guests were Hilda Mathison, John Sparrow and the W. J. Turners. During the mornings and most of the afternoon, Yeats stayed in his room. It was only in the evening that his vitality returned, when he would talk until midnight, charming us all by his fantasy, his wit and his ripe judgments of men and women, and by the shrewdness of his comments on poetry and life generally.

I thus described Yeats and Lady Dorothy at Penns in the Rocks [1] : "I sketched the two as they sat in the garden, the young and the elder poet ; Dorothy slight, fair, with deep violet eyes and auburn hair, with full arched lips, somewhat drawn down, a slight Elizabethan figure next to Yeats, dressed in crimson shirt, flowing coloured tie, now in his later years brown-skinned under his crown of white hair, his dark eyes aslant, broad-shouldered and ample of form, he, once so pale and lanky."

Hearing that his seventieth birthday was approaching, I consulted Masefield, and together we issued an appeal among Yeats's friends for a tribute to his eminence as a poet.

It happened at this time that a sale of J. P. Heseltine's drawings was to be held at Sotheby's. Among these were some early ones by Rossetti, and I managed to procure the very drawing which

[1] *Since Fifty.*   Faber & Faber.

E

would appeal to Yeats. Masefield, always generous with his time, went to Dublin to attend the Birthday Dinner and presented the drawing on behalf of his English admirers.

But his English admirers were not always quick to show the admiration they felt. When, in honour of his seventy years, Nancy Price put on three or four of Yeats's plays at the Little Theatre, the small house was half empty.

Some time previously, I put forward Yeats's name as a candidate for the Athenaeum, when he was at once elected under Rule II. Pleased at the compliment, he jibbed at the entrance fee. Later, the fee was abolished for members so elected, and I drew attention to the difference this was likely to make in Yeats's decision. He was re-elected unanimously and at once accepted membership. Heretofore, during his visits to London he had stayed at the Savile Club : now he made the Athenaeum his headquarters. He appreciated the company there, knowing, too, he could be undisturbed when he wished to be alone.

In his later years Yeats tended more and more

to get away from anything in the nature of aesthetic gesture. Speaking of painting he quoted his brother Jack as saying that he painted to please himself. " This," he said, " is not my attitude to poetry. You must remember your audience ; it is always there. You cannot write without it." He held the reaction against tradition to be tiresome. We have to accept the conditions we find in our own time ; within their discipline we can still remain free enough to be ourselves. Not that he had patience with easy acceptance ; wherever there is thought there is opposition. He wanted to inspire the youth of Ireland with the national ideals to be found in Berkeley and Swift. A return to clarity, to the poetic expression of what is in the minds of the common people. He aimed to have his poems sung in the streets. Yet there are obscure passages in many of his later poems.

In one of the last letters I had from him he wrote :

I wish you would find some way of making a drawing of Maude Gonne. No artist has ever drawn her, and just now she looks magnificent. I cannot imagine anything but an air-raid that would bring her to London. She might come to see the spectacle. Do you ever go to Dublin?

Alas, he himself was not to return to Dublin. His failing health made it advisable that he should winter in the south of France. From there he wrote on December 29th, 1938:

My dear Rothenstein,

You advised me two or three years ago to get some embroidery designs from Diana Murphy. I asked her for four large designs. She has done three and all are beautiful, and I suppose the fourth will come sooner or later; but I want something rather different now. I want another mind and I want one or two small designs (say 18 inches by 12). My sister, as you know, was the pupil of William Morris and May Morris and is probably the only one left now. She is trying to do a series of needle pictures which represents incidents or symbols of the Irish heroic age. Miss Murphy has done the Land of Youth as it is in my early poetry, a design from a poem of mine called *The Happy Townland*, and an *Innisfree*. The idea of these designs and of one she is now doing is to picture an ideal country. I want one or two heroic incidents possibly from my poems, familiar themes. I will of course send suggestions, probably from the old epics. In England the romantic movement is of course over and the average artist guys the dream. With us it is the opposite. Some of the best known of the young men who got themselves killed in 1916 had the Irish legendary hero Cuchulain so much in their minds that the Government has celebrated the event with a bad statue. For us a legendary man or woman must still be able to fight and to dance. Now, do you know of some young artist who would do one or two designs for me and not be too expensive? I know this is making a great claim upon your time but I have been trying everywhere in vain.

Yours ever,

W. B. YEATS

Yeats had been struck by some imaginative drawings which my son Michael had shown him. I suggested therefore that he might like Michael to try his hand.

Would your son care to do a design [he wrote on January 3rd, 1939] for embroidery for any of the following poems of mine? *Byzantium, Sailing to Byzantium* or *The Wandering of Aengus*? . . . The poems I have selected are all well known to the public and I think it will be more easy to sell a design if it suggests a poem and the poem suggests it.

Three weeks after writing this letter his heart failed him.

It is for others to estimate Yeats's genius as poet, prose writer and playwright, his commanding figure in the Irish literary movement and in that of the theatre. I can only pay tribute to his inspiring company, his fecund speech, his aristocratic attitude towards art and life. Above all I think of his intellectual hardihood, of his sure gallantry in defence of courageous initiative, of outspoken opinion. He had, too, the striking appearance and imposing character we associate with genius; these accentuated his faults as they did his qualities. There are few shoulders fitted to carry the mantle he wore so proudly throughout his ardent life.

IV

THE MAN AND THE DRAMATIST

BY LENNOX ROBINSON

I. THE MAN

I WAS IN WALLA-WALLA, IN THE EXTREME west of the United States. I had arrived early after travelling all night. I lectured to a college in the morning, then followed a public lunch, there was to be another lecture in the afternoon, an evening reception, a play, a midnight train to Denver — all this in connection with Ireland and the Abbey Theatre. I stole an hour in the afternoon and rested on a hotel bed. The inevitable telephone rang : a young man from the college wanted to see me. He appeared, the editor of the college magazine. He wrote poetry and left with me a few good poems. But he said :

" Have you ever met Mr. Yeats ? "

" Yes, he has been my best friend for twenty years or more."

" You have spoken to him ? "

" Of course."

The young man was speechless, captured by an emotion.

How obviously the Browning poem springs to mind ; I, too, have " seen Shelley plain ".

I met him first when I was twenty-two and he was just twice that age. I suppose it was only a young man's impression (I was very inexperienced for my age) but he seemed then to be a middle-aged, if not almost an old man. This is strange, for he kept his appearance of a young man till he was over thirty, perhaps he suddenly put on maturity. At any rate by the time I met him he had an air of great dignity and authority, a poise not a pose. He was often, all through his life, to be accused of being a *poseur*. It was not the case. He had mannerisms of movement and speech as every person of great individuality is bound to have, his pose would have been to try and pass himself off as an ordinary person. He was extraordinarily striking in appearance, tall, slim and his hair still quite black, the beard of earlier years had disappeared. His eyes were strangely placed, one of them was always weak and by the end of his life its sight had gone. This made it forgivable in him to pass a friend in the street without recognition or to fail to identify people in a crowded room. He has talked to me for an hour about the Abbey Theatre, calling me by the name of a previous manager, and then he suddenly stopped, looking at me as if he had only just realised my identity and appearance (yet no two appearances could be in greater contrast than the former manager's, and mine); there followed an apology which did away with any feeling of hurt on my part, for he was always courteous and gentle save when roused to vehemence on some matter of vital importance. In dealing with his inferiors there was no arrogance, no consciousness of superiority, and anyone who ever served him quickly grew to love him.

I have said that when I met him first he was slim; that was not always the case. He could vary, and vary rapidly, from leanness to stoutness. I used to tell him he was like the moon that waxed and waned. He was a very moderate eater and drinker — the most rapid eater I have ever met, and took pains about his figure, doing exercises of some sort to keep himself trim. Up to a few years before his death he could look on occasion extraordinarily young, look like that lovely Sargent drawing done just about the time I met him first, and his appearance at the end of his life can only be described by the one word — noble.

In some obituary notice he was described as unapproachable, and the writer said that no one outside his family ever called him by his Christian name. This is not the case. To his intimate friends he was " Willie ", to his close acquaintances he was " W. B." In his early days in the Theatre he was known (but I am sure only behind his back) to players and staff as " Schoolboy Yeats ", perhaps because of his big black tie knotted in a drooping bow which might suggest some schoolboy's uniform. Certainly, in the last years, for me he was always " Willie " to his face ; in speaking of him to his friends one generally used his initials.

In his early years he affected the big tie,

loosely knotted, the correct wear of a poet of the
'nineties. Then he became more orthodox. He
liked clothes and liked them to be correct. He
took me aside once in the early days of our
association and told me that a gentleman didn't
wear a " made-up " dress-tie. I protested that
mine was home-made. He apologised, but a
year afterwards he warned me again, and again
I protested, but from that time forward was
always careful that my tie should be slightly
awry. Cats he loved and birds, the wild birds
that would be fed at his windows or the canaries
in their cages, and he would write quite undisturbed by their flood of song, but it distressed
him that they *would* use their bath-water for
drinking purposes, and he sought vainly from a
bird-fanciers' shop for a cure for this deplorable
habit.

He was never a rich man, for most of his life
he was a very poor one and he had to be careful
of his money. He was a good man of business
and advised me as a young man never to waste
my time over trivial journalism ; if everything
was written with care, in a year or two there

might be enough to gather into a book of essays. That he had followed this path himself was proved when Mr. Horace Reynolds unearthed contributions to American papers written by him as long ago as 1887, republished forty-seven years later, which make good reading. He loved beautiful things and a beautiful way of living, but he had to deny himself. He was never mean but he was never extravagant, he dared not be; after all, most of his friends were as poor as himself, so it was not very difficult to live simply.

In reading his poetry, at any rate when he was reading it to two or three of his friends, his voice was musical and without affectation. He did not boom the verse as A.E. did nor croon and chant as James Stephens does. When he was speaking in a large lecture-hall or over the wireless he became a little affected and too deliberate in his speech, and a record that the B.B.C. possess of his reading of *The Lake Isle of Innisfree* is not characteristic of him at his best, yet there are tones and cadences in it which are entirely his own.

An " unbuttoned " Beethoven is often spoken of ; there was no unbuttoned Yeats, either in his work or in himself, and that is why I deny that he was guilty of pose. He loathed pretentiousness in others and so had none himself. He preferred the *News of the World* to one of the more pontifical Sunday papers : in the former he said, you might read " a murderer's last words, in the latter, not the last — alas, not the last — words of So-and-so's high-falutin' dramatic criticism ".

The only art to which he was almost wholly insensitive was music, and musicians as a body he quite unreasonably disliked, though one or two of his best friends were musicians.

I am not musical, I have the poet's exact time sense, only the vaguest sense of pitch, yet I get the greatest pleasure from certain combinations of singing, acting, speaking, drum, gong, flute, string, provided that some or all of the words keep their natural passionate rhythm.

He once told me that he composed all his poetry to either of two airs and he hummed them to me. I could make nothing out of them, not even a rhythm. But in later years he seemed to be developing a musical sense and described rightly George Antheil's music for *Fighting the Waves* as " most strange, most dramatic music " though it committed the crime he had so often denounced, the giving of many notes to the same word ; as he admitted himself, " I have gone over to the enemy ". He liked Mr. Arthur Duff's music to *The King of the Great Clock Tower*, — again, music with a strong rhythm — and, probably influenced by his friend F. R. Higgins's knowledge and love of Irish folk-tunes, some of his latest poems seem to show that he was writing with a definite Irish air in his head.

He was the most brilliant conversationalist I have ever known, at once witty and profound. At its lightest his talk was full of anecdote and reminiscence, and if he could fail at times to recognise a friend or a face he had a meticulously accurate memory of facts. His sisters have told me how time and time again, turning up some old letter, they have verified some tiny fact, some insignificant incident which had taken place many years before and which he had written or spoken of with perfect accuracy of date and occurrence. It was dangerous to argue with him on a question of fact, he was certain to be right. You might hear him tell the same story over a number of years, the story never varied, each detail was the same, the very language in which it was narrated unaltered. He could rejoice in telling a Rabelaisian story but, ten to one, if you tried to cap it he grew disgusted. It is maddening that my memory is not like his and that of all the fine talk I have heard from him so little remains. In argument his mind worked very quickly, and having him and George Moore to supper one night in London after the theatre — they were not the best of friends then — it was delightful to sit back and listen to poor Moore fumbling for the retort that was to annihilate ; but before the right words could be found Yeats had presented some other facet of the subject, leaving Moore floundering in the background.

F

II. THE DRAMATIST

IT is a commonplace, facile thing to say that
Yeats as a dramatic poet was a failure. Failure
in what respect ? Certainly he did not realise
his dream of the creation of a verse-theatre in
Ireland or have a success in Ireland and outside
it with his own verse plays. But that failure is
due to the taste of the public here and elsewhere,
not to his failings as a dramatist. If we admit,
as we must, that there is a very small audience for
his plays, for what modern verse-plays is there
an audience ? In evidence of the growing
degradation of taste he used to recall the enor-
mous popular audiences for poetic drama in
ancient Greece, and those other audiences still
comprising thousands — the Elizabethan period ;
today only a couple of hundred can be gathered
together out of London's millions to listen for
a performance or two to any verse-play that is
not by the Bard.

Yet the Theatre (always, I think, the most obstinately conservative of the arts) is slowly learning from cinema and music and lighting. There is some faint stirring in its bones. The cumbersome " set " stage has become more mobile ; we dramatists are able to visualise scenes on it we could not have dreamed of twenty years ago, we are now not afraid to throw ourselves on the imagination of our audience and to suggest a complete scene by a few lines scrawled on a back-cloth. We are not afraid, on occasion, to use the audience as part of the play and to build our stage right out into its midst. All these are freedoms and improvements in our technique which make easier the writing and production of non-realistic plays — and verse, though it may deal with a railway-strike, cannot be other than non-realistic. But we cannot yet claim that there is a large audience in English-speaking countries for the verse-play.

By such an audience I mean people who will go to see *any* verse-play, either for the excitement of judging a new work or for the interest of seeing the revival of an old one, just as the real lover of the prose theatre will go and see any play " on the chance ". Lacking such an audience, the dramatic poet must fall back on the few lovers of verse who will be content to gather in a drawing-room, a garage or an old barn. The first man to realise this stark modern fact was Yeats.

Admitting the failure in our own time of the poetic play let us imagine that there is an audience for such a drama, and then ask ourselves what place Yeats would have in its repertory ; whether he is a poet who has merely split his narrative poem into speeches and given them to different characters and named the result a play, or whether his work has faced all the problems of the prose dramatist and emerges from the contest a play and yet in verse.

The first thing a dramatist needs is a good subject. A play comes to a dramatist's mind as a situation or as a character, but they depend on each other : character implies situation, there can be no character without situation, and a situation is empty until filled with characters. Yeats had almost always an unerring eye for situation.　A very pure and holy woman sells her soul to the Devil to save many other souls ; a father, unwittingly, kills his only child ; the powers of Evil steal away a girl's soul and her life ; a poet starves himself for his ideal ; a husband murders his wife's lover ; a play-actress makes herself a queen ; the unbeliever, at the moment of death, tries to find God ; the spirits of Swift and Vanessa appear at a modern séance ; the mysteries of Calvary and of the Resurrection — these, in a few words, are the themes of his greatest plays.　Each of them is a simple dramatic anecdote, admirable substance on which to build a play.　That one can sketch the subject matter in such a few words almost proves the fact.

Having found his subject the dramatist must determine his point of attack, the moment in the story at which he enters.　Yeats arrived at this point unconsciously and was surprised and excited once when I talked to him for a long time on this subject, pointing out how Ibsen in his last, most mature plays chose to enter his subject at a later and later moment, so that everything that matters most in such plays as *John Gabriel Borkman* and *When We Dead Awaken* has taken place years before the curtain rises, the plays are a turning-over of cold stones in an extinct volcano. The dramatist knows his characters from the moment of their birth, knows their parents and grandparents, but he dare not hark back to them at any length as a novelist can easily do ; he is all the time faced with what Henry James called " the tyranny of the clock ". Shakespeare perhaps pondered whether *Hamlet* should begin with the murder of the King. It is the proof of the supreme dramatist that the point at which he enters his subject seems always to be the right, the inevitable one, and we do not stop to question it or him. *Hamlet* seems. to begin at the perfect moment.

Having chosen, consciously or unconsciously, his point of attack, the situation must be established as rapidly as possible, the characters related to the situation and to each other, set out like pieces on a chess-board. The dramatist is working against time — the tyranny of the clock — so everything said or done must have bearing on subject and character, no hares must be started and left unchased ; a play is a progression from situation to situation.

It is very rarely nowadays that a writer starts a drama without some knowledge of stage technique. He has, at any rate, read or seen a number of plays. If he is lucky enough to have been born in the United States of America and to have gone to a university, he will probably have had the opportunity of attending a play-writing class, or, in his university theatre, will have had the chance of studying play-production, acting, scenery and stage-designing. Yeats had not those opportunities, and his first two plays — *The Countess Cathleen* and *The Land of Heart's Desire* — were written (he says) " before I had any practical experience, and I knew from the performance of the one in Dublin in 1899 and the other in London in 1894, that they were full of defects ". Elsewhere he says : " The act was written long ago when I had seen so few plays that I had pleasure in stage effects ". Probably his play-reading was confined to the Elizabethan dramatists ; he several times said to me almost apologetically that the only dramatist he really cared for was Shakespeare. Also we must remember that when he began to write for the stage in the early 'nineties, the London theatre was not the place to attract a person of culture and intelligence. The tide was to turn within a few years, but was to bring on the crest of its wave the kind of plays Yeats least cared for — Ibsen and the early Shaws and the early English realistic work. His only equipment at the beginning was his great gift of verse, and two fine themes, — one " the most impressive form of one of the supreme parables of the world ", the other a more tender and fanciful anecdote. We shall note later how imperfect was the first version of *The Countless Cathleen*, but how quickly, having seen a few performances and grown interested generally in the stage, he seized on his play's defects, righted them and finally made it the perfect, triumphant thing it is.

During the early days of the Irish Theatre he worked hard at production, producing not only his own plays, but, with Lady Gregory, the other plays in the repertory. Ten years later, when he made me Manager and Producer of the Theatre, his only reason for doing so (I had no technical qualifications) was that I had written a promising play or two, and a dramatist should know his instrument. Consciously or unconsciously he knew that he himself had learned his instrument in those years of producing, and he was now putting a beginner to school. By the time I came to the Theatre, in 1910, the days of his great verse-plays were over, but I made the first production in Ireland of *The Player Queen*, some of the Plays for Dancers, *The Words upon the Window-Pane*, *The King of the Great Clock Tower* and *Resurrection*, and his two translations from Sophocles. With the exception of the first play, which was produced during his absence in England, while not actually producing them, he took an active part in their rehearsal. Strange to say, he had not many, perhaps had not any, theories about the speaking of verse. He hated any affectation of speech ; chanting or crooning would drive him frantic, his ideal verse-speaker should have a rich and varied voice and the sense of acting that evokes those qualities. These things come only from constant practice in verse-speaking, practice which makes verse come as naturally from the lips of the player as does prose. If he never got in Dublin the theatre of poetry he had dreamed of, it was not for the want of a few very good verse-speakers — I instance Frank Fay and Sara Allgood — and others who were potentially good ; the theatre of his dream failed because the Irish theatre took a different, a realistic path. But that theatre had been founded to be a National Theatre, a mouthpiece for the young writers of Ireland; he had never intended it to be his particular play-thing, and when the young writers turned away from poetry, he more and more as the years passed allowed his own work to be put on one side. Lady Gregory might plead, I might plead, it was of little use. He had an artist's pride ; he knew he could only rely on an audience which would be polite but indifferent to his work, which would count the moments until the curtain fell on *Deirdre* and rose again on some peasant comedy or some tragedy dealing with an event very close to their own life. Later on, he was to make his own theatre for his peers.

But in rehearsal, if he did not spend much time on the speaking of his verse, he paid great attention to other things — emotion, movement, scenery, dress and lighting. He would spend half an hour getting some movement or piece of " business " to his liking and would cry out in passion — never in temper — at some clumsiness of mine or on the part of the players. To them and to me those rehearsals were a joy and an inspiration, for he brought to bear on the play an instinct and an intelligence vastly superior to our own. He was completely lucid in his explanation of what he wanted from our players and producer, but nearly always demanded something beyond our capacity ; and he would patiently try in this way and that way to get his desired result.

The *décor* of the early plays must have been very bad. Even still, rummaging through the Abbey wardrobe, one comes on costumes made for the Yeats plays more than thirty years ago, many of them actually stitched by Miss Horniman. They are incredibly graceless and ugly, clumsy material cut skimpily and often bordered with mock fur which would not tempt a puppy. Years were to pass before Charles Ricketts designed noble costumes for *The King's Threshold* and *On Baile's Strand* and before Mr. Gordon Craig designed costumes for *The Hour-Glass*. From that time there was no looking backward, and Edmund Dulac, D. Travers Smith and Norah McGuinness were called on to design for the Plays for Dancers, and George Antheil or John Larchet or Arthur Duff must make the music. Mr. Dulac as well as designing the costumes for *The Hawk's Well* also wrote its beautiful music.

Yeats's theories of production can be found in *Plays and Controversies* and elsewhere. This note to *The Green Helmet* sets down very simply his aims in the production of a poetic play ; it illustrates his producer's eye, that eye which must be all-seeing :

We staged the play with a very pronounced colour-scheme, and I have noticed that the more obviously decorative is the scene and costuming of any play, the more it is lifted out of time and space and the nearer to faery-land we carry it. One gets also more effect out of concentrated movements — above all, if there are many players — when all the clothes are the same colour. No breadth of treatment gives monotony when there is movement and change of lighting. It concentrates attention on every new effect and makes every change of outline or of light and shadow surprising and delightful. Because of this, one can use contrasts of colour, between clothes and the background or in the background itself, the complementary colours for instance, which would be too obvious to keep the attention in a painting. One wishes to keep the movement of the action as important as possible, and the simplicity which gives depth of colour does this, just as, for precisely similar reasons, the lack of colour in a statue fixes the attention on the form.

He took pleasure, as every good dramatist and producer should, in stage effects but he almost apologises for his taste.

We have made a prison-house of paint and canvas (he wrote) where we have as little freedom as under our own roofs, for there is no freedom in a house that has been made with hands. All art moves in the cave of Chimaera, or in the garden of the Hesperides, .

or in the more silent house of the gods, and neither cave, nor garden, nor house can show itself clearly but to the mind's eye.

Later, in 1912, speaking of *The Countess Cathleen*, and of *The Land of Heart's Desire*, he wrote :

They are, I think, easier to play effectively than my later plays, depending less upon the players and more on the producer, both having been imagined more for variety of stage-picture than variety of mood in the player. It was, indeed, the first performance of *The Countess Cathleen*, when our stage-pictures were made out of poor conventional scenery and hired costumes, that set me writing plays where all would depend on the player.

But, while writing of him as man of the theatre, I must not forget that his interest was not only in the production of his own plays. After watching the performance of a realistic play he would make a dozen criticisms, heart-searching to producer and players. I had hung the pictures too high, the farmer's daughters were too clean (" Smear cow-dung on their faces ! " I remember him exclaiming) ; some actor's wig was atrocious, the scene was too darkly lit. Our supposedly "good" furniture was undistinguished, therefore he and I must spend a couple of afternoons visiting old furniture shops in Dublin, picking here and there some genuine period piece and so accumulating a complete set of Georgian furniture. He took pains, as a good producer should, over the smallest "prop." He was eager for experiment in the theatre, and seized on the idea of the Gordon Craig screens ; he seized on Mr. Granville-Barker's idea of a squared stage-cloth for use at rehearsal. His was our Peacock Theatre and his our School of Ballet, and had we not been always poor, and he a good man of business, he would have been prodigal in what he spent on the stage.

As an illustration of his skill as a dramatist I want to analyse rather carefully his first and his longest play, *The Countless Cathleen*. We must judge the play by the final version of 1912, but it is extraordinarily interesting to compare that with those of 1892, 1895 and 1899. In the twenty years between 1892 and 1912 he had learned his stage. We may quarrel with amendments made to some of the early lyrics, but there is no alteration of importance to quarrel with in this play. " The goddess has never come to me with her hands so full that I have not found many waste places after I had planted all that she had brought me."

What situation has the dramatist to establish at once in this play, this *Countess Cathleen* ? Famine, and with famine despair of God. We see a peasant's hut, a father, a mother, a son — Seumas Rua, Mary and Teig. In the first two pages of rapid dialogue Teig makes clear to our eyes that " the land is famine-struck. . . . What is the good of praying ? Father says God and the Mother of God have dropped asleep." Against Father's and Son's un-faith shines Mother's faith, and, that established, the Countess Cathleen, her nurse Oona and Aleel with his lute come in. Cathleen is in a half-dream, seeking for some forgotten childhood's haunt where she was happy long ago. All day as she has wandered she has given money to the starving poor ; she empties her purse now and leaves, still wrapped in a dream which has grown troubled. The Demons, disguised as Eastern merchants, enter, the snare is set, they spread their gold on the table, but it is not there for charity's sake, it is there for barter. Though the starving peasants have sold all their possessions,

> They have not sold all yet.
> For there's a vaporous thing— that may be nothing,
> But that's the buyer's risk— a second self,
> They call immortal for a story's sake.

Seumas and Teig without hesitation are ready to sell their souls, and the obvious end to the scene would seem to be the striking of the bargain, and in that way the first version did end. But the skilful dramatist will always try to dovetail one scene to another and leave his audience guessing and asking themselves "What happens now?" Yeats realised this, and very soon the changed act ended with no purchase of souls ; Seumas and Teig have first to earn their price as the Demons' agents ; they have to cry at every cross-roads that there is money to be had for souls, and they rush from the scene, carrying our imagination with them on their errand.

Thus, in fifteen minutes' playing-time, the scene of the whole play has been set and the chief characters established. The nurse Oona, though she is only given a few lines (she was more richly written in earlier versions) is plain to our eyes, so is Aleel. Oona used to pipe in her old woman's broken voice, " Who will go drive with Fergus now ? " instead, Aleel sings in his rich young voice, " Impetuous heart be still, be still." The scene is tight and dramatic, a masterpiece of construction.

In contrast, after a swift scene such as that, the dramatist can afford a few minutes of relaxation and so the second scene — set in a wood — begins in a mood of meditation, with the Countess still in a half-dream vaguely listening to Aleel's pagan remembrances. He sings the lovely :

> Lift up the white knee.
> That's what they sing,
> Those young dancers —

(Ballet in the old days of the Empire Theatre had not attracted Yeats ; but after the Russians had

visited London, this lyric, he told me, was
inspired by it.)

But the nostalgic mood is rudely broken, the
Steward arrives with tittle-tattle of robbed
gardens ; quick on his heels Seumas and Teig
come running, crying out the market for souls.
Cathleen who has just said that " there is no
soul but it's unlike all others in the world . . .
and therefore none whose loss were less than
irremediable " wakes from her dream and becomes a creature of action. Her questions to
the Steward are clean-cut, her orders precise.
All her possessions must be sold, she must outbid the Demons and fetch from across the sea
ships laden with cattle and corn. Her house
must be a refuge for the old and ailing, from this
time forward she will have nothing of her own.
The earth " burns her feet ", she hurries away,
the scene ends in excitement ; again our imagination is driven forward asking " What happens
now ? "

Quiet again. The scene is the hall of the
Countess's house and Aleel pleading with her to
flee from the evil days that he feels are coming,

from the terrible death that he foresees is awaiting her. She refuses to go, though she scarcely knows why she stays. Aleel leaves her, she passes into her oratory ; the Demons come, break into her treasure-room and steal her treasure. She comes back and for the first time find herself face to face with the Demons. We know them for what they are, but she does not, a fact that heightens the tension of the scene. She suspects them.

> There is a something, Merchant, in your voice
> That makes me fear. When you were telling how
> A man may lose his soul and lose his God
> Your eyes were lighted up, and when you told
> How my poor money serves the people, both —
> Merchants, forgive me — seemed to smile.

The Demons go before they have quite revealed themselves, peasants rush in ; they have heard strange noises as of robbers in the house, Oona is wailing with the news that the treasure-house has been rifled and all the gold that was to outbid the Demons is gone. And then the great theme unfolds itself, the ultimate tragedy, the theme the author called " the most impressive form of one of the supreme parables of the world " ; Cathleen arrives at her great resolution ; she herself must sell her soul for the sake of others, she must make the descent into eternal Hell ; and the act ends with her great cry of abandonment :

Mary, Queen of Angels,
And all you clouds on clouds of saints, farewell.

The very brief fourth scene is intended to be played in front of a cloth in order to give time to change and set the scene for the final act. In matter it simply consists of a procession of peasants on their way to sell their souls, talking of the gold they will get ; and, though tricked out by a repetition of Aleel's song, it is too short — the only unsatisfactory thing in the play.

The final scene is drama from the first moment to the last. The Demons are pressed for time. Though the Countess is penniless, the money she obtained from the sale of her possessions has bought grain and cattle ; they are on the high seas, only three days away. We are back in Seumas Rua's hut, Mary lies there dead, she has starved herself to death rather than eat food bought by Demon gold. The Demons sit bartering for souls with a crowd of peasants and the talk is full of character and bitter comedy. The Countess enters and in spite of the peasants' protests she bargains away her soul. She asks an incredibly high price, not only in gold but in the freedom of the souls already bought. She signs away her hope of Heaven with a quill-pen plucked from the cock of Peter, and as she signs, her heart begins to break, and she staggers from the scene. In an early version, her dead body was carried back by spirits singing that lyric which will be found in *The Rose*. Yeats first named it " The Countess Cathleen in Paradise " and later " A Dream of a Blessed Spirit ".

> All the heavy days are over ;
> Leave the body's coloured pride
> Underneath the grass and clover,
> With the feet laid side by side.

In the ultimate version, the peasants carry her in, still living, still able to speak, but within a few moments she dies. All then is tumult and confusion, darkness and thunder, and at the last a vision of angels.

> The light beats down ; the gates of pearl are wide.
> And she is passing to the floor of peace,
> And Mary of the seven times wounded heart
> Has kissed her lips, and the long blessed hair
> Has fallen on her face : the Light of Lights
> Looks always on the motive, not the deed,
> The Shadow of Shadows on the deed alone.

The producer must use the version of the last act, given in the notes to the play ; it has the essential swiftness. The other version is too clouded with Irish mythology. I know no scene of action in the modern verse-theatre that can match this for intensity and great poetry, and the man who can read it and say Yeats is not a dramatist, is a fool.

I have dwelt on this play at some length to emphasise its almost faultless construction. I shall not dwell on its poetic quality except to say that among the early work it must be taken as the most perfect example. It is before his " embroidered " period, or, if it be decorated, subject and setting seem to call for such a treatment, and the wonder is that so much of the verse is unelaborate. Happening to read some old and hostile criticism of this play and of *The Land of Heart's Desire*, I was surprised to find them labelled as decadent and Maeterlinckian. The characters in them are precise and accurate, the motives behind their actions are clear-cut and definite, the scenes are easily identified, and we know why the characters are there. M. Maeterlinck's plays, beautiful as so many of them are, are shadowy and vaporous. With him, we must wonder and guess and puzzle things out for ourselves ; but there is no puzzlement in Yeats.

Passing from this play of many scenes, consider Yeats as a writer of one-act plays, in which form, indeed, most of his dramatic work was cast. People ignorant of stage-writing are apt to imagine that a one-act play is three times easier to write than a three-act play ; in reality it is five times more difficult. The concentration, the foreshortening of incident and character, has got to be intense. An anecdote — which my dictionary describes as " a narrative of detached incident " — easily lends itself to such treatment, and therefore there is nothing to wonder at and note in the construction of *The Land of Heart's Desire.* No background, no past history need be limned in, the characters can quite naturally unfold themselves, they need but to be contrasting types to give interest to the story. In spite of the beauty of its verse *The Land of Heart's Desire* is an empty, superficial little play which captivates the ear for a moment but goes no deeper. Again, as in *The Countess Cathleen,* the theme is the struggle for a soul, but whereas we are passionately concerned with Cathleen's self-imposed doom, we can only feel Mary to be a foolish, selfish young woman ; and, to speak brutally, her husband is well quit of her. We find it difficult to believe in the authenticity of the Faery's spell, or that the Priest should be so powerless, and we are not surprised to read that very soon the author " had grown to dislike it ".

But *Deirdre* (written in 1906) is a very different matter. Here is a theme which is no anecdote, here is a traditional Irish story, one of the great, well-known Irish stories which has a beginning, a middle and an end, a narrative stretching over a number of years. The theme can be told in a few words. The High-King of Ireland, Conchubar, rears a young girl to be his queen; before their marriage she flees with a young man, Naisi; they wander for seven years in Scotland; enticed by Conchubar's promise of forgiveness they return to Ireland and Naisi is murdered. Some forms of the legend have it that Deirdre kills herself at once, others that she becomes Conchubar's unwilling wife and, later, throws herself under his chariot. The end, at any rate, is tragic.

The theme obviously presents itself as a three-act play. In that form A.E. saw it in 1902, in that form Synge wrote it years later. Yeats took the harder way, in 1907.

He naturally takes as his point of attack the final tragedy, and begins his single act where A.E. and Synge started their last acts. But though he is using a story well known to many of his Irish audience, he must make it clear to anyone who has never heard of the Irish Helen. He must rapidly and apparently effortlessly give us the background, set the scene, define the characters. In *On Baile's Strand* he had used characters — Fool and Blind Man — whose main purpose was to describe the situation and the dramatis personae ; but, except for one scene with Cuchulain, they are extraneous to the action. In *Deirdre* he makes the chorus — let us call it that — an integral part of the play; the three wandering women musicians are on the stage all the time, they are spoken to, and they speak in reply. In four speeches, the first musician pictures the three principal characters (it is a play of only four characters). The fourth, old Fergus, Conchubar's foolish friend, who cannot be brought to believe in the King's treachery, enters to the musicians before their reminiscence can become tiresome and unreal. His speeches explain himself and further amplify the story. The women have the foreknowledge of their kind, they have seen strange, armed men gathered, seen a marriage-bed prepared, its curtains stitched with the miracle-working stones that have power " to stir even those at enmity to love ". But before they can do more than hint at these things to Fergus, the lovers come in, Naisi gay and confident, glad to be back in his native land, Deirdre filled with doubt, suspecting treachery ; and when Fergus and Naisi have gone out, the musicians have nothing comforting to tell her. Conchubar's promises are empty ones, mere " hackles on the hook ". They are to be murdered ? No, worse. Naisi is to be slain and Deirdre brought in triumph to the King's house. We begin the play in a mood of vague apprehension ; with every moment, as the treachery unfolds itself, the pace becomes more rapid and more terrible. No need to dwell on Deirdre's attempt to make Naisi escape while there is yet time, no need to dwell on the weapons of argument she uses, some false, some true ; Naisi is murdered and Deirdre kills herself.

Yet it is not enough just to remark on the play's perfect — one dare not use a lesser word — construction, and to note that, given an even adequate performance, it cannot fail to be a stage success. But the reasons for its success, apart from its poetry, need to be examined. When I say that the pace, the feeling of apprehension, grow more and more terrible, that is not to say that the play is a race of emotion from beginning to end. A moment comes when Naisi at last realises the King's treachery, knows the house is surrounded and there is no escape. Then he becomes " calm, like a man who has passed beyond life ". We have had Deirdre's vain beating at the bars, we have now Naisi's more noble acquiescence. They'll play at chess till Conchubar's men come, Naisi will hold them from the doors to the last moment and when that comes give Deirdre " a cleanly death with this grey edge ".

Yeats had said that after his first two plays he had written more for variety of mood in the characters than for stage-picture. He misjudged himself. Being the good dramatist he was, he could not avoid stage-picture. He had the artist's innate desire for colour and costume and, with the exception of two early peasant plays (and even *Cathleen ni Houlihan* is in the costume of the eighteenth century) and *The Words upon the Window-Pane*, all his work is decked out with costumes of some bygone time, with masks, with strange musical instruments, with unrealistic settings. *Deirdre* is placed in such a setting, a guest-house in Conchubar's wood, the costumes are of the heroic age, the murderers are black men. Variety of mood there is in plenty, but he heightens our excitement by a dramatist's devices. One of the excitements in the theatre is for the audience to know something, some terrible threat, some treachery unknown to the players ; it is this which, at a melodrama, makes a gallery audience instinctively cry out and warn the heroine that the villain is hiding behind the curtains. There is a tremendous moment in *Deirdre* when she is pleading with Conchubar for her lover's life ; unseen by her, the King makes two signs to the black slaves who are holding Naisi tangled in a net. The first sign, and he is gagged ; the second, and he is silently huddled behind a curtain to meet his death, as we well know. But Deirdre continues her pleading, which has grown to us now unbearably poignant, because useless. The King laughs ; Deirdre speaks :

> You laugh.
> Yes ; you are laughing to yourself. You say,
> "I am Conchubar— I have no need of him."
> You will cry out for him some day and say,
> "If Naisi were but living "—(*she misses Naisi*) —
>   Where is he ?
> Where have you sent him ? Where is the son of Usna ?
> Where is he, O where is he ?

This is a moment of supreme drama.

There is another moment of somewhat the same sort. Deirdre has taken a dagger from the Musicians, unknown to all in the play but them and her. We, the audience, know it, and after Naisi's death she asks the King, before she goes with him to his house, to allow her to pay her last respects to the dead. It is better for Conchubar, she says, that her last memory of her lover be that of a soiled and bloody man and not the comely shape of the young man she loved. We know her intention is to go behind the curtain where Naisi lies and join him in death. Conchubar suspects as much.

> How do I know that you have not some knife,
> And go to die upon his body ?

We catch our breath. But Deirdre, drawing herself up, stakes everything upon her answer :

> Have me searched,
> If you would make so little of your queen.
> It may be that I have a knife hid here
> Under my dress. Bid one of these dark slaves
> To search me for it. *(Pause)*

CONCHUBAR : Go to your farewells, queen.

Yeats used to say about Deirdre's performance — " Red-heat up to Naisi's death, white-heat after he is dead " ; but indeed she has more than two moods. Apprehension, terror, despair, lying to Naisi in an attempt to save him, lying to Conchubar to win her own death, and one lovely scene with Naisi of reminiscence and love. It is a great part for a tragic actress ; alas ! that I never saw Mrs. Patrick Campbell's performance — but Maire O'Neill's is unforgettable. Every part in the play is roundly written, every part has its variety, and of the one-act verse-plays it is the most supremely satisfactory.

Yeats admired beyond measure Synge's *Deirdre of the Sorrows*, written a few years later than his own play ; he called its last act " the most poignant and noble in Irish drama ", and to many people its prose speech, so full of Irish idiom, seems the most fitting medium in which to treat an Irish heroic theme. There is hardly an Irish country word in the whole of the Yeats *Deirdre*, hardly an Irish turn of phrase. Its language is in the great tradition of English blank verse ; the songs sung by the women have no relation to the Irish countryside ; it is, in spite of its subject, very little Irish. But it and *The Countess Cathleen* demonstrate his superlative stage-craft.

All the dramatic values that are in *Deirdre* are to be found in *On Baile's Strand*. Many will prefer this play above all his others ; at one time it was certainly the author's favourite. It is harshly male. Not only are there no women in it (save the half-human singers), but the play seems to pass before us to the clash of steel on steel, masculine arrogance matched to masculine arrogance. Where the tragedy in *Deirdre* is feminine and poignant, the tragedy in *On Baile's Strand* is grim ; the one is set in leafy woods, the other on the edge of the harsh sea ; it is *Macbeth*, not *Romeo and Juliet*.

As in *Deirdre*, the "Chorus"—in this case a Blind Man and a Fool—outline the story. They do it at greater length than in *Deirdre*, they speak in prose, they are definitely Irish characters. The anecdote of the play is of the simplest; there are but three characters who matter, Cuchulain, the High-King Conchubar and a Young Man. Conchubar is an old man, cautious, with many children to succeed him. Cuchulain is many years younger, impetuous, wild of blood, and though he has been the lover of many women, believes himself childless and boasts that he leaves

> No pallid ghost or mockery of a man
> To drift and mutter in the corridors
> Where I have laughed and sung.

But his boasting is pretence, for in sleep he cries out bitterly, "I have no son".

We know from the Chorus that a young man has landed on the shore, that he has defied the guardians, refused to tell his name, and killed a man. But the Blind Man knows who he is — the son of Aoife, the great fighting Queen whom Cuchulain once mastered in the North. I have been wrong in saying there is no woman in the play, for Aoife is there although she never treads the boards and speaks no word. She is the evil influence in the action, and by touch after touch, allusion after allusion, Yeats makes us see her as clearly as if she stood before us. She is one of those " cross queens that live in hungry Scotland " ; Cuchulain recalls her " stone-pale cheek and red-brown hair ", the " high, laughing, turbulent head of hers thrown backward, and the bowstring at her ear ",

> None other had all beauty, queen or lover,
> Or was so fitted to give birth to kings.

She hates Cuchulain who has defeated her in battle — the only man who ever did so — and she brings up her son to kill him. Cuchulain and the Young Man meet, his name is still unrevealed, he is only known to be from Aoife's country. Cuchulain is under bonds to the High-King to fight the stranger and drive him from the country. But he sees in the Young Man the same tint of hair, the same stone-pale cheek ; he does not wish to fight him, he would have him as his friend — he knows not why ; and he cries out that he will fight any man who fights the stranger. Conchubar forbids the friendship and Cuchulain actually lays hands on the High-King, but is horrified and dazed at his own action ; and in a frenzy he turns on the Young Man, and all rush out to watch the combat. When Cuchulain returns wiping the blood from his sword, it is to meet the Fool and the Blind Man. The Blind Man tells Cuchulain that he knows what mother the Young Man had ; he was a queen's son. What follows is dramatic dialogue at its highest pitch and it must be quoted :

CUCHULAIN : What queen ? What queen ? (*Seizes Blind Man, who is now sitting on the bench.*) Was it Scathach ? There were many queens. All the rulers there were queens.

BLIND MAN : No, not Scathach.

CUCHULAIN : It was Uathach, then ? Speak ! speak !

BLIND MAN : I cannot speak ; you are clutching me too tightly. I cannot remember who it was. I am not certain. It was some queen.

FOOL : He said a while ago that the young man was Aoife's son.

CUCHULAIN : She ? No, no ! She had no son when I was there.

FOOL : The Blind Man there said that she owned him for her son.

CUCHULAIN : I had rather he had been some other woman's son. What father had he ? A soldier out of Alba ? She was an amorous woman — a proud, pale, amorous woman.

BLIND MAN : None knew whose son he was.

CUCHULAIN : None knew ! Did you know, old listener at doors ?

BLIND MAN : No, no ; I knew nothing.

FOOL : He said a while ago that he heard Aoife boast that she'd never but the one lover, and he the only man that had overcome her in battle. (*Pause.*)

BLIND MAN : Someone is trembling, fool ! The bench is shaking. Why are you trembling ? Is Cuchulain going to hurt us ? It was not I who told you, Cuchulain.

FOOL : It is Cuchulain who is trembling. It is Cuchulain who is shaking the bench.

BLIND MAN : It is his own son he has slain.

To one who knows the play well it is difficult to say at what point the audience realises that the Young Man is Cuchulain's son. We have here again, as in *Deirdre*, the audience in possession of a dreadful knowledge of which the protagonists are innocent. We have here again the piling up of apprehension in a play of excitement and action which grows in intensity from moment to moment — an almost perfect example of Yeats's stage-craft.

His dramatic work falls easily into two or three categories, and the semi-final category, that of the Plays for Dancers, needs careful consideration. But before passing to them, two plays should be noted. The first is *The Hour-Glass*, which in the early version (1902) became at once a popular play. But in this form it soon ceased to give its author pleasure.

The early version of the play, which was only too effective, converting a music-hall singer and sending him to Mass for six weeks, made me ashamed, but I did not know till very lately how to remedy it. I had made my Wise Man humble himself to the Fool and receive salvation as a reward, but now I have given it a new end which is closer to my own thought, as well as more effective theatrically.

This version was first played in 1912 in a beautiful scene and costumes designed by Mr. Gordon Craig, and this is the version which should always be played, even in preference to the more complicated verse-version of 1914.

The other to be considered is *The Player Queen* — a most delightful, most annoying and most unsatisfactory play. It has a lovely, fantastic idea, and bristles with characters ; but for once the author's constructive skill seems to have deserted him. The " point of attack " does not seem to be indubitably right. Should the story not have begun earlier, should it not have been in three acts or in five ? The first act — the play consists of two acts in prose — does foreshadow the second, but fails to excite our interest ; the characters amuse us but we are not particularly concerned in their fate ; we have very little inkling of what the play is about. There are glorious rambling speeches by a drunken poet, a vile story about a queen, a strange old man with an itching back who is looking for straw to roll on ; that is all. The second act is more pertinent, all the scenes among the company of players are amusing, excellent and authentic — did not Yeats know well the nature of actors and actresses ? — and again every new character,

Queen, Player Queen, and Prime Minister, is full of life. Yet in the end one feels cheated. A grand comic situation has been created, the play is full of colour and life, but we do not need the author's own word to know that there is a philosophic idea behind the play which is never allowed to rear its head. Farce no less than tragedy can be a vehicle for philosophy. There is no one noble in this play, no Cuchulain, no Deirdre ; but there is portrayal of character ; we have for hero a drunken poet, for heroine a torment of an actress. Subsidiary persons in others of his plays, what actors call "character parts", had nearly always been written in peasant dialect, and for that dialect — he readily admits the fact — he had depended on Lady Gregory. Hence come Blind Man and Fool in *On Baile's Strand*, hence the Cripples and the Mayor in *The King's Threshold*. Yeats delighted in character and oddity, and would tell many a story with oddity as its subject, but such stories seldom had for their subject Irish country-people, or if they had, they came probably at second-hand from Lady Gregory. *The Player*

Queen shows how much better, with how much more originality and strange fun, Yeats could have written such characters had he been left to himself ; and if other proof is needed, it is to be found in the old man in his last play of all, *The Death of Cuchulain*, written after Lady Gregory's death. The invention there is all his own and therefore entirely satisfactory.

I need a theatre ; I believe myself to be a dramatist ; I desire to show events and not merely tell of them ; and two of my best friends were won for me by my plays, and I seem to myself most alive when a room full of people share the one lofty emotion.

This cry was wrung from him in 1916 ; it had been in his thought for years that there was no popular audience in Dublin or London for verse-plays. Henceforward for more than ten years he was to invent a theatre for himself and the few people who could share his " lofty emotion ".

He found his model in the aristocratic theatre of Japan. In that year, 1916, he published, through his sister's Cuala Press, Japanese plays by Fenollosa, translated by Ezra Pound, and to this book he added a long essay on the art of that theatre. In the same year *The Hawk's Well*, the first of the Plays for Dancers, was performed in a London drawing-room. His imagination was profoundly stirred by the Japanese plays, and more stirred by the masks and head-dresses and costumes designed for his play by Mr. Edmund Dulac. He saw in this kind of play " a certain possibility for the Irish dramatic movement ", and hoped in them " to have attained the distance from life which can make credible strange events, elaborate words ". Such plays could be played in a room " for so little money that forty or fifty readers of poetry can pay the price and have no need of mob or press to pay their way ". He freed himself at one sweeping gesture of most of the mechanism of the Western theatre.

In place of it a new mechanism had to be substituted. The stage must be on the same level as the audience, any large ordinary room would serve for a theatre ; a chorus, entirely detached from the players, would " call to the mind's eye " scene and characters ; masks would be used in place of make-up ; music would be used and dance where it was necessary, and strange beautiful costume. The movements would be stylised and perhaps accompanied by drum-taps. But, in truth, the new mechanism of non-realism was seldom carried to its extreme ; he asked for a backcloth painted with waves for *Fighting the Waves*, and if D. Travers Smith's was not like that which Mr. Harker would have been ready to supply, that was only a difference in paint and personality. In the same play a bed has to be used with real curtains which can be drawn across it. The sheepskin in *The Cat and the Moon* must be a real one, and black at that. In *Calvary* there is a " practicable " cross, and dice for the soldiers. To have carried his invention to the uttermost extreme, he should have used puppets ; disguise and make artificial as much as you will with mask and stylised movement, human flesh and blood will out, unreality put on reality and call for a real stick to hobble with, a bed to lie on.

Yet, having pointed out that the unreality of these plays is not so unreal after all, there is no denying that they brought to the stage a new, strange and beautiful convention. Dr. Gordon Bottomley speaks of the excitement elicited in him and in the audience who saw the first production of *The Hawk's Well* in London ; when the play was given some ten years later in Yeats's drawing-room in Dublin, the same excitement was manifest ; an excitement that did not fade in an hour but lasted for days. Of those four first Plays for Dancers, this is the most perfect, perhaps because Yeats was working with only one collaborator, Mr. Dulac, who wrote the music as well as designing masks and costume. The knowledge that a famous Dutch sculptor, Hildo Krop, had designed masks for the second of those plays, *The Only Jealousy of Emer*, led to Yeats making a prose version of the play (though preserving the musicians' lyrics) ; and by some happy chance — if chance there be — meeting George Antheil one night in some Paris café, I suggested to him (though I only knew his music by reputation and a pianola version of his *Ballet Mécanique*) that he should compose the music. The result was, as Yeats wrote of it, " Antheil's most strange, most dramatic music ", which beautifully suited Krop's powerful masks. By this time we had at the Abbey Theatre our own school of ballet with a County Dublin girl as its principal, Ninette de Valois, famous as one of Diaghilev's ballet ; and these four creatures of genius, Yeats, Krop, Antheil and de Valois, created a most dramatic result. But the play, as rewritten, had passed beyond the range of a drawing-room ; it was intended for an ordinary stage. The mechanism of the Eastern theatre was already beginning to prove inadequate, nor could " forty or fifty readers of poetry " pay its price, for its augmented orchestra and its ballet made it a production too expensive for frequent revival in our impecunious theatre.

From 1922 when Yeats came to live in Dublin and became a Senator, his mind dwelt more and more upon eighteenth-century Ireland. As a Senator he took his duties very seriously, speaking only on subjects on which he had special knowledge or on subjects about which he felt passionately. He assisted in obtaining our beautiful and distinguished coinage, helped to shape the Copyright Act, spoke vehemently on divorce. He was utterly fearless in his opinion, his position by this time in the world of letters made him unassailable in the little Irish newspaper world. Now it was that all his deepest reading was in the great eighteenth-century Anglo-Irishmen — Swift, Burke and Berkeley, and Croce and Gentile who owed much to them. His political, philosophic thought of those years, we may call them roughly the last eighteen years of his life, can be found in his introduction to *The Words upon the Window-Pane*, contained in *Wheels and Butterflies*, one of the finest essays he ever wrote. He was now reading Swift for months together, " Burke and Berkeley less often but always with excitement, and Goldsmith lures and waits " ; his main thought was concerned with " that one Irish century that escaped from darkness and confusion ". And from this thought sprang *The Words upon the Window-Pane*.

It was first produced at the Abbey Theatre in November 1930 and it is an astonishment. It is in prose, the prose of middle-class modern Dublin life. Though written in Lady Gregory's house and dedicated to her, it seems to show nothing of her influence ; instead, he draws on his experiences of spiritualistic séances, when the medium is some ignorant, poor woman.

The scene is laid in a room in an eighteenth-century lodging-house, in the room of the medium, Mrs. Henderson, which is reputed to have a vague connection with Swift and Stella.   Some words are dimly scrawled on a window-pane ; tradition says they are Stella's, and one of the sitters, a Cambridge student, writing a thesis on Swift for his doctorate, recognises them as being from one of her few poems.   Before the medium arrives, in talking to the other sitters, this speaker recalls the Swift mind, the Irish eighteenth-century, the Yeats mind.

" I hope to prove [the young man says] that in Swift's day men of intellect reached the height of their power — the greatest position they ever attained in society and the State, that everything great in Ireland and in our character, in what remains of our architecture, comes from that day ; that we have kept its seal longer than England. . . . His ideal order was the Roman Senate, his ideal men, Brutus and Cato.   Such an order and such men had seemed possible once more, but the movement passed and he foresaw the ruin to come, Democracy, Rousseau, the French Revolution ; that is why he hated the common run of men. ' I hate lawyers, I hate doctors ', he said, ' though I love Dr. So-and-so and Judge So-and-so ! that is why he wrote *Gulliver*, that is why he wore out his brain, that is why he felt *saeva indignatio*, that is why he sleeps under the greatest epitaph in history. You remember how it goes ? It is almost finer in English than in Latin : ' He has gone where fierce indignation can lacerate his heart no more '."

The séance begins ; the " control " is a little girl, called Lulu, who died when she was five or six years old, and speaks through the medium in a babyish voice. The sitters endeavour to call up one dead friend after another, but in vain ; some presence, some terrible old man dominates the séance. It is Swift, talking in his harsh man's voice, and answered in a moment by Vanessa. Later he speaks to Stella and though she never speaks, the impression of her presence is so vivid that I have heard many people after witnessing a performance speak of the actress's representation of Stella ; they would hardly believe me when I said that that character never spoke. I shall not dwell on the exact plot of this most moving tragic little play, I only dwell on its superb craftsmanship. Every dramatist must be furious with himself that he had not thought of the device of making an actress enact many characters. One does not forget Miss Ruth Draper and her imitators, but if one has been at a séance, and heard a medium under control, a young woman, speaking naturally in a cultivated English voice, changing in an instant to a rough man's voice speaking the broadest Somerset, and a few minutes later speaking in voluble French (of which language she had in natural life only the most rudimentary knowledge) and a few minutes later in fluent German (of which she had no knowledge) one must realise the terrific dramatic possibilities of such a conception. And every actress must long to play that medium's part — so excellently played by Miss May Craig — and be in one half-hour, Mrs. Henderson, Lulu, Swift and Vanessa.

There is more to praise in the stage-craft of the play than the invention of the medium ; the dialogue at the beginning before the entrance of the medium is an excellent piece of exposition,

I

it interests us, and quickly sketches out the persons, making each a very individual character; and before it has time to weary us, the séance begins. Then, lest we weary of it, the séance breaks and we are for a few minutes back in normality, only to resume again the séance, more highly intensified. The end is terrible and dramatic.

Years before, in his preface to those plays of Fenollosa, Yeats had guarded his enthusiasm for their form by saying that he might "turn to something else later". In *The Words upon the Window-Pane*, in *Resurrection*, in *Purgatory*, plays of old age, he turned back to the theatre of his youth. He could use drum and dance and mask if his subject called for them, he could use a suburban sitting-room or an upper chamber in Judea with equal ease. "I need a theatre; I feel myself to be a dramatist"; the cry haunts us as the thought haunted him. He need have made no such protest, no such plea. In play after play from *The Countess Cathleen* all down the years, he had proved his mastery over his instrument, testing it, developing it, learning from it, and teaching it to obey.

V

THE POET AND THE ACTOR

BY W. G. FAY

It is a strange fact that though there is plenty of evidence in the history of the Gael of a high degree of culture in the arts of oratory, music and poetry, yet there is none of the use of drama as a means of expressing the national ideology. There is none in Scotland, nor in Ireland — even in the myths and legends — and there is none in Wales. It was not until the opening year of the twentieth century that plays were written in Gaelic and performed by Irish people, when Cumann Na nGaedeal produced Father Dineen's *Tobar Droidheachta* (" The Magic Well "), at the Ancient Concert Rooms, in Dublin. In October 1901 for the first time a play in Gaelic was produced in a theatre, when *Casadh an Sugán* (" The Twisting of the Rope "), by Douglas Hyde, now the President of Eire, was played by members of the Gaelic League in the Gaiety Theatre, Dublin. At about the same time W. B. Yeats, with Lady Gregory's help, founded the Irish Literary Theatre for the purpose of producing in Dublin plays written by Irish authors, or on Irish subjects. The Literary Theatre was responsible for seven productions — plays written by Irishmen and played by English actors of good standing.

The poet's first experiment in play-writing was in verse, with the title of *The Land of Heart's Desire*. It reads much better than it plays, owing, not to any fault of the author, but to the impossibility of making the fairy child — on whom the whole story depends — appear to the audience as anything but what she is — a very human little girl. Yeats's next play was *The Countess Cathleen*, the story of a beautiful woman who sold her soul during a famine to save her people from starvation. It met with a very mixed reception on theological grounds, in spite of excellent production and a first-rate cast.

Yeats's main interest in the Theatre at this time sprang from the attempt of some among the younger poets to establish in London a society of people who were supporters of the new drama, both in prose and verse. With the co-operation of other artists, they succeeded in forming the Stage Society, which was the means of giving performance to the work of a number of dramatists who have since become famous, including George Bernard Shaw. The romantic drama that, for the preceding century, had been the mainstay of both dramatist and actor, was beginning to feel the opposition of the new naturalistic school of play-writing. This was a movement that had spread from Norway over the rest of Europe, and needed a different technique. Engagements became fewer for actors trained to speak Shakespeare or the old comedies, who used an English that was entirely free from local colour, whether of the Universities or of Mayfair. Such stars as Barry Sullivan, Herman Vezin, Edward Compton and Henry Ainley were not only great actors but were great orators as well, each able to carry the weight of a whole play on his own shoulders. Any one of them, when performing a verse play, whether by Shakespeare or another poet, could hold an audience so spellbound that it failed to notice that the supporting company was often anything but first class, or that the scenery was sadly in need of the attention of the scenic artist. The fall of the curtain often brought a dozen " calls " from an audience that had risen to its feet to applaud — a sight never seen in the theatre today. But it was evident to all writers using verse as their medium that, when this generation of actors had passed from the stage, there would be none who had been trained to follow them, and to this day they have never been replaced.

The greatest lyric poet of our time was too wise not to foresee that soon it would be useless for poets to write for the theatre, unless a pro-vision were made to secure a continuous supply of actors capable of speaking verse. He began a search of the London stage for artists who could be relied upon to treat a poet's lines with respect, and not to follow the advice of a prominent producer, " Make prose of it, my boy ! " When *The Countess Cathleen* was about to be pro-duced, the most difficult part to cast was that of Aleel, the poet, and Yeats was asked to try a young actress whose name was Florence Farr.

In her performance of Aleel he found for the first time an artist who could deliver verse with feeling and understanding fine enough to satisfy the wishes of the most exacting poet ; and Yeats was not easily pleased ! She had a voice of great charm, and like the poet himself, she was interested in mysticism. To her he confided his idea of trying to form a company of players specially trained in verse-speaking, with perhaps a remote possibility of finding somewhere in the suburbs of London a very small theatre, where performances of poetic plays might be given, gradually creating an audience interested in the speaking of verse. If Antoine could induce an audience from Paris to come up to Montmartre to see his Grand Guignol plays, surely, Yeats thought, it was possible in the city of London to find enough people to support one small theatre devoted to staging the work of the poets! It was not ! A theatre might have been found without great difficulty, but the necessary financial help was not forthcoming, and without it Miss Farr could not face the difficult period that would have to be gone through while collecting a company of players and training them in the new technique that she and Yeats had evolved. It is possible to get money to subsidise any other form of art either here or in America, but as yet no English-speaking country thinks that the Theatre is worth it, excepting the small annual payment made by the Government of Eire to the Abbey Theatre in Dublin.

If there was but little interest in the Theatre at that time, there was a great deal in music, and this caused a revival of the works of the composers of the seventeenth and eighteenth centuries ; but unfortunately they lost much of their beauty when played on modern instruments, instead of on those for which they were written. Arnold Dolmetsch, a young musician who was both an enthusiast for old music and a versatile instrumentalist, thought it should be possible, after a little experimental work, to construct modern models of the old musical instruments. In the course of a couple of years he succeeded in making copies of the harpsichord, the spinet, the clavichord, the psaltery and others. Then he gathered a small orchestra of musicians interested in old music, and at one of his concerts Yeats and Miss Farr heard, for the first time, music played on the psaltery, a stringed instrument of the zither type. It occurred to the poet that such an instrument could be used to accompany the speaking of verse, and that a notation, similar to that used in music, might be invented for the timing and cadence of the words of a poem, to be spoken while they were accompanied by chords struck on the psaltery. The matter was discussed with Dolmetsch, and at his suggestion he made a special instrument of simpler design that could be played like a small harp, allowing the speaker to stand upright, and light enough to be held in one hand. After some practice Miss Farr became quite expert in using the psaltery. As an accompaniment to the spoken word it helped to give to the listener a key to the cadences used by the poet when he created the poem the speaker was reciting. Miss Farr's voice and oratorical power gave to lovers of poetry a pleasure of the same kind as that which a great singer would give to lovers of music.

But Yeats had not at that time realised the difference there is between words written to be read in a printed form and words that an actor has to memorise and afterwards vocalise. In the first case there is no intermediary between the creative poet and his reader, but in the second between the writer and his audience there intervenes the actor or speaker, whose personality, for good or ill, may affect the listener's interpretation of the author's meaning. There are many writers who find it impossible to put their ideas into words that come " trippingly off the tongue ", though their works run trippingly into many printed editions. But by the time Yeats reached his dramatisation of the story of Deirdre, he had completely mastered this difficulty ; for in that play the verse is as easy to speak as that of Shakespeare or Dryden.

When the time came that Miss Farr's professional contracts were too numerous for her to continue giving attention to the development of the new method of speaking poetry, it was carried on by Miss Maud Gonne, a close friend of the poet, living in Dublin. She had not Miss

Farr's technical skill nor her experience of playing before an audience, but she had a natural gift for reading poetry, and combined a fine voice with a magnetic personality. To Yeats's verse she gave a vitality that has not been equalled since. As president of the " Daughters of Erin ", the women's section of the Sinn Féin, she was helping Arthur Griffiths to establish branches of the organisation all over Ireland ; and to help her work she asked Yeats to write a play that would embody the ideals for which Sinn Féin was fighting. In response he wrote his first prose play in one act, and called it *Cathleen ni Houlihan* — one of the symbolic names for Ireland. Written with all the skill of a great lyric poet, this is a very fine propaganda play about the old woman, Cathleen, persuading young Michael to leave his family and his sweetheart, to follow her along the weary road that leads to the Calvary that all must reach who attempt to help Eire — from Robert Emmet to Michael Collins. With Maud Gonne playing Cathleen in a play specially written for her, success was a foregone conclusion.

Cathleen ni Houlihan was the first modern Irish play presented by an entirely Irish cast, and its success led to the founding of the Irish National Theatre Society, with Yeats as president. He had come to feel that unless Irish plays were played by Irish actors, as well as written by Irish authors, they failed to produce in performance the atmosphere that gave them their distinctive national character. Through his observation at the Stage Society in London, William Poel's Elizabethan Stage Society, and other similar movements, his experience enabled him to give both help and encouragement to this little group of Irish actors who were striving, against great odds, to invent a new technique that, while simple, should be also dramatically effective.

There was no demand for Irish plays other than those known as melodrama, and the few writers in Ireland who were willing to try their prentice hands at play writing had little idea of the limitations of drama as a medium compared with the novel. The Irish National Theatre Society soon became the Mecca of all Irish writers who could string dialogue together and call it a play ; it was then forwarded to the unfortunate reader for the Society, who generally discovered that the " play " would take only three minutes to perform, or had twenty scenes of a minute each, and each in a different location. It was a lucky chance that brought Yeats and J. M. Synge together at a friend's house in Paris. If the meeting had not taken place, Ireland might have lost her greatest dramatist, for, having written *The Tinker's Wedding* in a rough scenario form, Synge found it impossible to finish it. Very quickly he learned from Yeats how to arrange exits and entrances, to keep his dialogue crisp, that long speeches slacken a play's playing pace, and the many technical details that are essential if a play is to be presented to an audience. When Synge came to live in Dublin, he spent much of his time in the Society's rehearsal room in Camden Street, learning by practical experience how a play gradually takes shape, from the time when the actors first read their parts to the later time when they are letter-perfect, know their positions, and have learned the business that puts life into it.

On many nights there were long discussions between the actors and the authors after rehearsal on all kinds of questions about the technique of acting. Yeats's experience in London of the modern methods of play-production enabled him to advise the players as to the technique in use by the best actors in the West End — both such as was helpful, and such as it was better to avoid. The tendency of young actors to be so confidential on the stage that only those occupying the three front rows of stalls are aware what the play is about, was one of the things to avoid, no less than the vigour of those healthy old-timers who could tear a passion to tatters, in voices that brought showers of immemorial dust floating down from the " grid ". Yeats was wise enough to see what was of value in both methods, the old and the new, and broad-minded enough to encourage the players to use whatever technique would give those still immature actors the chance of reaching the goal of all performers, " holding the audience ".

While the Society was awaiting the advent of J. M. Synge and Padraic Colum, there was a great dearth of plays, and to help in filling the gap, Yeats wrote his only prose comedy, *The Pot of Broth*, a dramatised version of an old folk-tale of the tramp who sells to the farmer's wife a stone that will make broth, in exchange for the chicken she was boiling for dinner. This was a fine stand-by for a long time, with three good parts — those of the farmer, his wife, and the tramp : it was performed more than five hundred times, and was the first play to give that group of actors a training in a most difficult branch of the actor's art — comedy.

In the Lenten season of 1903, a close time for all Irish theatres in those days, Yeats wrote his only morality play, calling it *The Hour-Glass*, so that the players might have something to offer their audiences in the holy season. It is the finest of all morality plays, with the possible exception of *Everyman*. In it he wrote two splendid parts for the two best players the Society possessed at that time. The Wise Man was played by Dudley Digges, now starring with the New York Theatre Guild and at Hollywood ; the other part was that of the Fool, played by

Frank Fay. The Wise Man was a very difficult undertaking for a young actor who had little knowledge of mediaeval history, the schools of philosophy, or the disputations of the schoolmen who taught in them ; but the poet was an authority on those subjects, and taught Digges how to interpret the life of a teacher of that time, whose great learning had undermined his faith in the dogmas of his religion. The best speaker the Society had at that time, Frank Fay, gave a performance of the Fool which showed Yeats that at least one of the players had nothing to learn about the art of speaking. Their mutual interest in the subject started a friendship that lasted for many years, the one dealing with it as a creative artist who was a great lyric poet, and the other as a master at interpreting the written word and passing it on to a theatre full of listeners.

One problem which the producer of *The Hour-Glass* had to grapple with gave him much uneasiness, and that was how to dress Miss Maire Nic Shiubhlaigh, who played the Angel so beautifully. Angels are a devil of a proposition on the stage ! The conventional method was to envelop her in a long white night-gown, with large golden wings sprouting from her shoulder-blades, and place her behind an opening covered with gauze. This would have required a larger stage than we could command then, and even if it had been practicable, it would have spoiled the simplicity at which the Society aimed in all its productions. Yeats dressed her like an angel in one of Botticelli's paintings, with a brave gold nimbus. By using very restricted movements, she kept right in the picture and gave a splendid performance. It was more striking than any ordinary theatrical " effect " that we could have used.

The Hour-Glass is a short play, and as we wished our audience to have a full evening's entertainment, we persuaded our president to give a lecture. He chose as his subject " The Reform of the Theatre ", and in it gave an account of new methods of staging plays that were being tried by the younger producers in Russia, Germany, France and London. Of these the most remarkable were the innovations in stage lighting. It is uncertain whether the first person to break away from the old methods of stage lighting was Appia or Gordon Craig. Craig began his theatrical experience with his mother, Ellen Terry, under Henry Irving's management at the Lyceum Theatre, London, a theatre Irving had made famous by his spectacular productions of Shakespeare, going so far as to get help from members of the Royal Academy in the historical and archaeological details of his scenes. It is possible that experience at the Lyceum drew Craig's attention to the increasing tendency to over-emphasise staging, to the detriment of the actor. Storms became so realistic that the player was inaudible amidst the roars of thunder and the whistling wind. Often the stage was over-crowded with papier-mâché properties, and thronged with " extras " — such citizens or soldiers as the play gave excuse for. He saw that if the art of acting were to be saved, it must set about finding a new technique. He knew that others were experimenting with lighting and scenery on the Continent, but not one of them was, like himself, " a man of the theatre ", a producer, a designer, and a skilled actor. But he didn't get an opportunity to have a free hand in a production until Ellen Terry let him stage Ibsen's *The Vikings*, and followed it with *Much Ado about Nothing*.

These productions met with the reception given to any daring innovation on the London stage ; the critics were puzzled. But Yeats was not : for, at the Shaftesbury Theatre, he saw for the first time the method of staging a poetic play which he and Miss Farr had imagined as an impossible ideal ; he saw his ideal materialised as a piece of practical stage-craft. In his lecture on " The Reform of the Theatre " the poet exhibited a model theatre, made by Craig, showing a scene in the new style. It was a simple horizon cloth with some rocks and trees in the foreground, painted in monochrome, but lit in three different colours. For the first time it produced a feeling of atmosphere in stage light-ing. Later when, through the generosity of Miss Horniman, the Society came into possession of the Abbey Theatre, Dublin, the opening play was Yeats's *On Baile's Strand*, and in it we tried for the first time the new method of lighting and staging. Our finances were extremely limited and our equipment was not extensive, so the scene was made of curtains of unpainted jute, but when flooded with amber light they looked like cloth of gold. At the back centre were a pair of doors, nine feet in height, on which were hung six large round shields designed by Robert Gregory, and when the doors were opened to Aoife's son he stood silhouetted against a background of topaz blue, giving an effect of sea and sky, with an atmosphere that could never be obtained by paint.

While the experiments in the new staging were progressing, the teaching of verse-speaking was carried on daily by Frank Fay, and by the time the theatre produced Yeats's *Deirdre* the players could speak verse well enough to give us hope that one day we would realise the poet's dream, and have in Dublin a company of players who could give to verse the music that singers give to opera. That such a company never came into being is our misfortune. Yeats made a live Irish Theatre, as is generally admitted ; but it was never the Irish Theatre of his dreams.

VI

WITHOUT THE TWILIGHT

BY EDMUND DULAC

Even in our enlightened age, the poet and the artist are still " messengers from an unreal world " and Tradition and public feeling demand that they should carry about themselves an atmosphere of unreality. The Nineteenth Century, moreover, insisted on their being also a decorative anachronism, an echo of some past Golden Age. Hence the inevitable humbug, conscious or unconscious, the Wardour Street pageantry, the preposterous jumbling of familiar things under a dreamland limelight. Hence the sophisticated lives : one for the gallery, another for the privileged few the great man allowed to gaze at him without his stage make-up, and the less glorious moments when he put on his bedroom slippers.

There was nothing of that sort about Yeats. He conformed indeed to the Tradition, he gave his public a most delicately perfect picture of the

Poet. Only he honestly believed in the picture. He was one with a background that was never blurred by futilities, that even in friendly intimacy endowed with equal richness a humble or exalted object, a humorous story, a profound thought.

There is a difference between acting a part for the benefit of an audience and living it for the sake of one's soul.

He came into a room with slow, deliberate steps, his hand raised in a gesture between a salute and a blessing. He did not say : "Hullo ! How are you ? " Some resented it. The gesture of the hand, like the beautifully untidy hair, the large enamel ring, the subtle colour of shirt, tie and dress, were part of the picture. Only he lived in that picture with more consistency, more sincerity than many. The world of aristocratic beings, cultured, refined, linked by a certain elegance of expression, a certain ritualism of dress and behaviour, that he had once realised about him, he always thought he might find it again round the corner. The raised hand was part of the ritual. Part of the ritual also, his love of the village craftsman, the untrained performer — images in his mind of the times when art sprang from a more intimate contact between the artist and the hidden forces that shape our universe.

There was, of course, the business of the Celtic Twilight : mere pictorial mood that he outlived easily. Still, round the Cuchulains, the Deirdres, how little there is of the clap-trap inevitable with the Launcelots, the Guineveres, the nymphs, the shepherds ! The background in which it took its place as a stimulating conceit had a depth, a richness that the confectioneries of knights and Greek maidens never knew.

Nor were the more " mysterious " aspects of his landscape elaborated to impress, to produce an artificial atmosphere of strangeness. Astrological charts, occult figures, unutterable formulae : all symbols in which he put a considerable amount of faith. Yet not the unreasoned belief, half ignorance, half self-delusion, of the mystery-merchant who takes them at their face value.

To him they were an expression of man's

desire for evidence of some sort of order in the world, the synthetic interpretation of unknown, inexpressible laws, the hands of the watch that tell the time but cannot tell us what Time is. Signs round which he crystallised certain obscure emotions to give them a meaning, as the artist uses the precision of a shape to crystallise an undefinable mood. Algebra, sines, cosines, the square root of minus one : also points of emotional fixation. Let the mathematician have his fun with them. He is a rational, practical man. But when we have gaped in wonder watching him reduce universal laws to a series of emotions, he sends us away empty handed. Yeats played with trines and squares, Trees of Life, gyres and cones, and we go away with a bagful of rich and precious things.

If he was a dreamer his dream was not the self-indulgent illusion of the romancer who pins butterfly wings to lizards' backs to turn them into dragons, tricks out with extravagant tinsel a mirage of ancient or distant lands and is afraid to wake up.

Yeats never indulged in strangeness for the

sake of strangeness, that aimless castle-building which takes no account of proportion or relation in the piling up of its material. His imagination was under perfect control. His fantasy is neither sham nor fantastic. It has the quality of unexpected fitness that is inseparable from true invention. The element of surprise in his imagery comes from discovery, not from wonder. It functions in parallel. The thought is modulated in an unusual key, transmuted into a significant symbol ; an unforeseen richness is disclosed behind familiar things, as is disclosed the delicate tracery of gold and colours on those Javanese puppets of cut-out leather that had only shown as black shadows on a white cloth.

His method of work had nothing about it of the unreal or the spectacular. He hardly knew the ecstasy of the picture-poet who rattles off his lines in a frenzy of inspiration. A word, a phrase would find an echo somewhere in his thoughts. He would sit beating his knee with one hand, or walk about the room, his words measured to his pace, muttering them over and over again in a sort of incantation. And if the magic worked, if the word, the phrase awakened a particularly exciting train of fitting associations, he would set all this out in simple, ordinary prose. Elaboration in poem form came afterwards.

I, who know nothing of poetry, who dislike the conventions, the contortions of most nineteenth-century poets, found pleasure in the smooth natural structure of his verse.

Had he been the stereotyped romantic figure some wished, some feared he was, there would have been in his intellectual approach to his work, no change, no further search for ever greater simplicity. And there would have been no welcome for the new generation of poets who, by all the rules of convention, should have been anathema. But his welcome was perfectly sincere, I know it was. Yeats was much too guileless to be diplomatic. Their respect for him was equally real. The fact is that with symbols less recondite, with subjects more substantial in nature, their process of thought, their method of expression were closely related to his own. The quality of their curiosity was the same, if the

objects were different ; they were doing what he
would have done had he been born thirty years
later.

Read again the poems written in the last ten
years. How much of the conventional dreamer
is there left ? How much of the romantic
aloofness ? Yeats was certainly more detached
than most, but his ivory tower had many doors
and many windows all wide open on to life.
Nothing was neglected or despised. Only he
made a choice among the people and the things
that went by. And the tower was never lost
in the clouds. He never blundered in his dress
or in his gestures, he never missed a train, he
never fell into a pond, he never lost a precious
thing. In fact he was often more precise in his
actions — through, perhaps, some well developed
subconscious power of attention — than many
less romantic people. I have seen him return
from a long walk at night, in the country when
the sky was pitch black and the roads a network
of mud-pools, with his shoes spotlessly clean. I
was bespattered to the knees.

I have not been trying to show that Yeats was

just an ordinary man. He was not. But round the figure of a great man a legend grows. When he is dead, some wish to preserve it, carefully embellished ; some like to destroy it and make play with the bedroom slippers.

If legend is to be destroyed round the figure of Yeats, let the dreamer of fancies and the playboy perish.

As for the bedroom slippers, I doubt whether he had any unbecoming, unshapely enough to be worth gossiping about. His most intimate moments never touched even the fringe of triviality. He came closer, he spoke of his more secret preoccupations without losing any of the decorous nobility that pervaded the man, his background, his work.

Whatever we may think of the " picture ", let us keep in all its simplicity the clear outline of a figure that had soared far enough above the atmosphere of his period to be free from its humbug and its morbidity.

VII

YEATS AS IRISH POET

BY F. R. HIGGINS

IRELAND WAS THE MOULDER OF YEATS'S mind, as it eventually became the sounding-board for most of his verse and the great stimulating impact on his life. Throughout that intense life two men were his aristocratic heroes : John O'Leary and Parnell. On them he fashioned his heroic poise. For him one man typified the significant romanticism of Irish life ; the other revealed its tragic realism. Yeats was the child of Parnell's race ; the son by adoption of O'Leary's ; but O'Leary's people — the Gaelic people, who lived dangerously to die jestfully — were his first and lasting influence.

From boyhood W. B. Yeats intimately knew his romantic and pastoral Sligo ; later Clare-Galway became more attractive to the growing austerity of his mind. All through life his thought was never far from the West of Ireland. As a boy its quaint and adventurous folk, its grey fringes touching an uncharted world, were seen through "magic casements". His early verse — heavy with dream and frail reality — arises from these. That strange territory, that phantasmagoria, was his rich possession of poetry ; and for it the English critics very quickly claimed a Celtic kingdom.

Yeats had thought to create a sensuous, musical vocabulary, to marshal the Irish fragmentary beauties into a great literature, and indeed to give to Ireland a constantly artistic conscience through the medium of a poetic hierarchy. Until about 1907 all his achievements are towards that aim. Yeats, however, grew weary of his own ceremonial style — a style that seemed more concerned with cadence than content, of things imaged, as it were, through water. And away from that poetry of ornamental illumination, rather than flash, he hardened himself, subduing the lavish painting and toning down the rich rounds. He sought to rid himself of elaboration, of redundancy — through various ways. He found his new method by ballad-writing, for instance, and by writing out first in prose the substance of the verse on which he was working. He, however, succeeded mainly in his later work by the introduction of and tenacious adherence to stern theme and structure. With that success his poetry of mood gives way to his poetry of dramatic passion. It became hard-bitten : more Gaelic in feeling.

This change of his is due surely to what he heard and knew of Irish verse, traditional and translated, due possibly to the influence of Lady Gregory's mind and Synge's, as well as to a dramatic command and understanding of his craft. His early interest in bringing back poetry to its spoken majesty — a poetry as much for the ear as for the eye — was shown by his experiments in speaking verse to the psaltery. English poets were losing not only their ears but their mouths. They lolled their tongues in unmanly verse, seemingly anticipating the depression and defeatism of much verse in the England of today. Yeats was mainly interested in the lyric, in song. He had heard the ballad singers in fairs and markets crying out their pointed words of dramatic passion to catch and hold the ear of passing crowds. In street, field and kitchen Ireland was always singing in his youth, he recollected ; all the material for song was at his elbow. Ireland gave his splendid memory the songs of the folk ; his friends gave him their translations from the Gaelic — precise, intense.

Snatches of these songs and poems were always running through his mind. Their phrases enter many poems by him. I remember him telling me some years back that most of his poems were composed to some vague tune, some lilt. Indeed, when we were together, he sang in his own uncertain, shy way, some of these poems. Whenever these poems were again repeated, at later dates, he always sang them to the same halting lilt. All poetry, Yeats frequently said, was song ; and his *Oxford Book of Modern Verse* was largely compiled by him on that principle. In song-writing, Yeats took more than a literary interest. He wanted the songs of Irish poets sung among Irish people. In writing his own songs, we worked together welding his occasionally meandering words to Gaelic tunes. That exercise was latterly his constant delight

— an enthusiasm afterwards fructifying in our jointly edited volume of Broadsides made from Irish traditional songs, the songs of our friends, and our own songs. Convivial meetings of Irish poets should be the occasion for song production. It was a frequent idea ; for him the social gatherings of the Irish Academy of Letters should take place in the upper room of some Dublin public-house, where the poets present would sing their own work. Such gatherings did take place, songs were sung, including Yeats's — but not in an actual public-house. Poetry must be brought to the people by song.

Yeats had no melodic ear ; he could not measure words to musical stresses — he realised their significance, sought hard to employ them ; but they were not at his ready command. The older musical scales, the Irish gapped scale with its dramatic possibilities, interested him ; he abhorred the modern scale and the verbal contortions of concert singers. That very lack of a honied musical ear may have offered verbal compensation. It saves him, at worst, from an easy jingle of softly flowing sounds ; from the monotonous regularity of well-timed stresses. Indeed, his innocent offences against the laws of musical grammarians, his unconscious flaws in conventional melody, are responsible maybe for his curiously haunting harmonics in rhythm. These unexpected gaps staying his music, these hesitations in verbal sureness, dramatise his cadence. His carefully poised verse is tuned, as it were, slightly off the note. Throughout one listens as to a folk singer, in constant fear that the thin run of melody will break on the perilous top note — altogether a tantalising music and a very personal music. Indeed, the very complex personality of this poet gave distinction to everything he wrote. His most formal lines, the most prosaic statement of his, stick in the mind, due possibly to such twist of syntax. Apart from such distinctiveness, the world of his mind, his imagination, circled far above the limp imagination of Main Street. His poetry never saw eye to eye with the middle classes. The bloodlessness, the loose sentiment of middle-minded verse, was to him an abhorrence. There were, for him, only two commingling states of verse. One, simple, bucolic, or rabelaisian, the other, intellectual, exotic, or visionary. The middle minds lacked distinction, poise ; he had little interest or patience with them. To them his poetry may seem a beautiful secretion from a mind of aristocratic pedantry in which the insignificant is given an absurdly pontifical importance. Above them Yeats, however, nobly asserted his aloofness, striking home with a more telling, naked enterprise in Irish song — until he retired, as it were, into his own shell, but from there we hear the almost imperceptible music of a lost Kingdom.

From his wise, anecdotal memory, his sustained interest in Irish mythology and life — from these every quaint experience, passionate phrase or queer thought became grist to his creative mill ; while his own brooding on character gave an almost passionate importance to the commonplace. Yet Yeats stood abreast of his age — writing out of our realities and what to him was reality — most modern among moderns, without being modernist. And through all his works appears one clear image — the image of himself, up to the end eager, youthful, impressionable, in his fierceness or foible. I shall never know an Irishman greater than W. B. Yeats. For fifteen years I was acquainted with him ; for half of that time I knew him intimately as a close and constant friend : most generous, most frank, full of zest and humour, a magnetic personality, always arrogantly the Irish poet. The night before he left Ireland on his last journey we were together in his room, talking poetry as usual. The new poem *Under Ben Bulben*, on which he still worked, he again read for me. I was elated, yet curiously sad. After midnight we parted on the drive from his house. The head of the retiring figure, erect and challenging, gleamed through the darkness, as I looked back ; while on the road before me, my thoughts were still ringing with the slow powerful accents of his chanting :

> Irish poets, learn your trade,
> Sing whatever is well made,
> Scorn the sort now growing up
> All out of shape from toe to top,
> Their unremembering hearts and heads
> Base-born products of base beds.

Sing the peasantry, and then
Hard-riding country gentlemen,
The holiness of monks, and after
Porter-drinkers' randy laughter ;
Sing the lords and ladies gay
That were beaten into the clay
Through seven heroic centuries ;
Cast your mind on other days
That we in coming days may be
Still the indomitable Irishry.

VIII

A NOTE ON W. B. YEATS AND THE ARISTOCRATIC TRADITION

BY C. DAY LEWIS

IT IS CUSTOMARY TO SAY OF YEATS THAT
he was the last poet in the aristocratic tradition.
This, more than most critical labels, though
inadequately addressed, does deliver the goods.
Strictly speaking, no doubt, the aristocratic
tradition in poetry died when the system of
patronage ended, its conditions of life rendered
impossible by the Industrial Revolution, its dying
words flung back in its teeth by Lord Byron.
Yet the attitude of mind and the style in Yeats's
poetry are aristocratic, and equally we feel that no
poet will be able to write after that manner again.
If it were only a matter of style — of the cere-
monious, witty, arrogant tone of the verse — it
might be possible to say that Yeats was a poetical
sport or a deliberate researcher into a *temps perdu*,
and he could not have been a major poet. But the
style of the later poems particularly is so consistent with Yeats's attitude to life, both as a private

man and a public figure, that he cannot even at his most extravagant be accused of falseness.

How did it happen that in the twentieth century a poet could be both a realist and an aristocrat ? The answer is found, I believe, in Yeats's boyhood. The Englishman, whose aristocracy has not for a hundred years shown responsibility towards the arts or provided material for legend, will read *Reveries over Childhood and Youth* with a sense of being conducted through the shades of a Golden Age. It is a commonplace that Ireland, until the rise of the new middle class which "showed . . . during the nine years of the Parnellite split, how base at moments of excitement are minds without culture", and to a lesser extent even up to the triumph of Sinn Féin, still presented all the salient features of the eighteenth century. The Irish land-owning class, amongst whom Yeats lived his boyhood, were absurdly proud, were snobbish, hearty, prudish, often a bit mad ; but, unlike their English counterpart, they had not grown vulgar, decadent or dull. Impoverished for the most part, they lived largely on their pride and their memories, it is true : but they, no less than the peasants around them, were consumingly interested in people — an interest so passionate that it raised gossip to the formal intensity of myth.

The opening pages of the *Reveries* show us this society as seen through a wandering, indolent, yet selective and Tchehovian eye. There is the grandfather, William Pollexfen, whom the poet once saw " hunt a group of men with a horse-whip " ; who, on board a ship that was going on the rocks, " judging from some answer that the captain was demoralised, took over the command and, when the ship could not be saved, got the crew and passengers into the boats ", but, eight men being drowned in spite of his efforts, " suffered from that memory at intervals all his life, and if asked to read family prayers, never read anything but the shipwreck of St. Paul ". There is the uncle who, when Yeats was seven years old, called him out of bed one night " to ride the five or six miles to Rosses Point to borrow a railway pass from a cousin ". They were autocratic, these family heroes, both giving and demanding largely.

They were also eccentric. But their follies, never furtive or squalid, had the same romantic grandeur as their natural surroundings. One uncle " was a clever man and had designed the Sligo quays, but was now going mad and inventing a vessel of war that could not be sunk, his pamphlet explained, because of a hull of solid wood ". Another relative had designed a steamer : " It had been built on the lake and dragged through the town by many horses, stopping before the windows where my mother was learning her lessons, and plunging the whole school into candle-light for five days ".

This society was not only violent and odd. It was also exclusive. At a time when its English counterpart was opening up to anyone who had sufficient money to oil the lock, it still maintained a strong contempt for trade. My own grandmother, a Butler who was related to the Yeats's, was disowned by her family for marrying an Englishman, the head of a respectable firm of chemists : while Yeats himself rejoiced that he inherited " blood That has not passed through any huxter's loin ". This ex-

clusiveness shut out more things than trade.
Both Nationalists and Catholics were despised :
yet, though the Protestant landed class had no
use for Nationalism, they had even less use for
the English. They despised the English because
they were always grumbling and kept no decent
reticence about their private affairs. " My
mother had shown them to me kissing at railway
stations, and taught me to feel disgust at their
lack of reserve ". This attitude is agreeably
summed up in Yeats's anecdote about the skate :
" Because my grandfather had said the English
were in the right to eat skates, I carried a large
skate all the six miles or so from Rosses Point,
but my grandfather did not eat it ".

It was, of course, easy enough for these Irish
squires to despise trade and the English habit of
self-exposure. " My father explained that an
Englishman generally believed that his private
affairs did him credit, while an Irishman, being
poor and probably in debt, had no such con-
fidence." Similarly the fact that his neighbours
were probably even poorer than himself prevented him from envying wealth as well as from

boasting about it. Still, though its pride and sense of decorum excluded it from much, the Irish squirearchy drew a compensating vitality from the peasants to whom it was bound in a free-and-easy feudal relationship. The peasants and sailors, with whom Yeats spent so many of his boyhood hours, did more than fire his imagination ; they provided more than the mere illusion of a vigorous, stable society : to the child of a family that had owned both land and ships they represented component parts of a community which was indeed settled, gracious and heroic in its simplicity.

No wonder that the poet's first conscious ideal was to found a new school of popular poetry in Ireland. As a child he had lived among people who were possessed by superstition, in a country where legends were as exuberant, hardy and tenacious as brambles. On the one hand stood the half-mythical figures of his own ancestors, on the other the autochthonous beliefs of the countryside — the Sidhe, the Banshee, prophetic dreams and second sight, Celtic heroes, the teeming ghosts, the more unorthodox and officious spirits such as the one which guarded a buried treasure and "looked like a flat-iron" (a manifestation only equalled when, years later, Bernard Shaw appeared to the poet in a dream in the shape of a sewing-machine). This was all part of the "unwritten tradition" that Yeats hoped to use as a basis for a new Irish literature which should be popular in a truer sense than the verse of writers like Longfellow and Whitman, and at the same time more deeply rooted than the Irish political ballads.

The poet's childhood, then, was, on the face of it, a singularly fortunate one. It possessed both a sense of the past and the free delights of the present. Firmly founded and lightly balanced between the sea and the land, between sailors and peasants on the one side and the ancestral pride and morality on the other, it also derived differing qualities from the two branches of his own family. "The Yeats's were always very respectable", a Sligo barber told him : they were "very well-bred and very religious in the Evangelical way" ; and again, "It was a Yeats who spoke the only eulogy that turns my head. ' We have ideas and no passions, but by marriage with a Pollexfen we have given a tongue to the sea cliffs.' " The Pollexfens were "energetic, successful people"; they roamed the seas, behaved impetuously and unconventionally; one kept a hatchet at his bedside for burglars, another was reputed to cure horses by conjuring: but, one way or another, they all had the grand manner, as in Yeats's description of his uncle George: "My uncle had the respect of the common people as few Sligo men had it; he would have thought a stronger emotion an intrusion on his privacy. He gave to all men the respect due to their station or their worth with an added measure of ceremony."

Such was the aristocratic tradition which Yeats inherited, a tradition differently reflected in the several facets of his own family, and reflected again in the wider, more primitive community where a woman was remembered for her beauty, a man admired for his authority, his physical strength, his birth or his wildness, but where it was still impossible to buy either respect or a posthumous reputation for cash down. " I am delighted with all that joins my life to those who had power in Ireland or with those anywhere that were good servants and poor bargainers."

2

When we inquire how this tradition was developed in Yeats's poetry, we shall find that there were three chief forces which modified and shaped it — the influence of his father, the poet's own intelligence and sophistication, and the Irish history of his times.

John Butler Yeats, a painter of the Preraphaelite movement, introduced his son into a world very different from the simple, archaic, vigorous life he had known in Sligo. The effect of the Preraphaelites on the poet's early work has been discussed often enough : what is less commonly understood is the influence his father's ideas had upon his poetry. Yet this influence was clearly adumbrated in the pages of the *Reveries*, where Yeats writes of his father, " He did not care even for a fine lyric passage unless one felt some actual man behind its elaboration of beauty, and he was always looking for the lineaments of some desirable, familiar life ". And again, even more significantly, " We should write out our own thoughts in as nearly as possible the language we thought them in, as though in a letter to an intimate friend. . . . Personal utterance, which had almost ceased in English literature, could be as fine an escape from rhetoric and abstraction as drama itself. My father was indignant, almost violent, and would hear of nothing but drama. ' Personal utterance was only egotism.' "

They were both wrong, or right. For Yeats's later work is at once highly personal and intensely dramatic ; we feel the " actual man behind its elaboration of beauty ", while in poem after poem Yeats, like his father, seems to be " looking for the lineaments of some desirable, familiar life ". The personal utterance has become dramatic because it was so profoundly influenced by the remembered speech of those amongst whom he lived his childhood — a speech that was simple, passionate, objective and intense.

In other ways too John Butler Yeats affected his son. This sceptical, pugnacious, self-critical painter was an exacting father. " He was indignant and threatening because he did not think I rode well." He drove the boy through Latin lessons. " He terrified me by descriptions of my moral degradation and he humiliated me by my likeness to disagreeable people." His opinions were eloquent, unorthodox and violently stimulating. His own ruthless self-discipline in art could not have failed to impress itself upon his son. And Yeats paid tribute to him when he wrote, " Years afterwards when I had finished *The Wanderings of Oisin*, dissatisfied with its yellow and its dull green, with all that overcharged colour inherited from the romantic movement, I deliberately reshaped my style, deliberately sought out an impression as of cold light and tumbling clouds. . . . It is a natural conviction for a painter's son to believe that there may be a landscape symbolical of some spiritual condition that awakens a hunger such as cats feel for valerian."

By bringing Yeats to school in England and introducing him to the Preraphaelites, his father took him the backward step that was necessary, under the circumstances, for the leap forward. It was a backward step because it took him out of a heroic community into a society that was at the best self-absorbed and often merely precious, and later set him among the coteries at a time when he had already begun to wish

> To write for my own people
> And the reality.

It was a necessary step because, although the boy had perhaps enough passion, imagination and capacity for hero-worship to have made an epic poet in a different age within such a community as Sligo gave him, history and his own divided, introspective character would have stopped him from developing on these lines.

Instead, he grew sophisticated, self-critical, impatient, as any man may to whom his times do not seem to offer a subject that fits his talent. The impact of this sophistication upon his aristocratic tradition and the images of his youngest days is the key to a great deal in the poetry. It is, for one thing, the key to his particular kind of romanticism, of which I shall say more presently : for romanticism is what happens when the heroic begins to doubt itself — it is the heroic betraying its own loss of innocence by protesting too much.

This lack of conviction crops up in the earlier poems. Their wistful rhythms and autumnal colouring reveal the nostalgia of the exile :

> I made my song a coat
> Covered with embroideries
> Out of old mythologies. . . .

In these poems he was indeed embroidering upon the heroic figures which to his childhood and the peasants among whom he spent it had been so much more actual, more natural, more simple. For all his theories and self-dedication, this poetry is no more " popular " than, say, the mediaeval romances of William Morris. Compared with it, the songs of Tom Moore, a far less sophisticated poet though he wrote in as artificial an idiom, approach much nearer to popular poetry.

When in his later years Yeats played down the Celtic mythology and began to use the other side of his tradition — the ancestral, aristocratic figures of his childhood and the friends of his youth — there is no longer any lack of conviction. But here again sophistication and intelligence have left their mark upon the material :

> A serving-man that could divine
> That most respected lady's every wish
> Ran and with the garden shears
> Clipped an insolent farmer's ears
> And brought them in a little covered dish.

Of Mrs. French, " gifted with so fine an ear ", as of other characters in these poems, we may say that she is all very fine, but she is no longer a purely heroic figure. Passion has left them a little, and irony crept in to make up the deficit. Though they amuse and satisfy, there is an air about them — as about certain noblemen and officials in Tchehov's stories — of faint distortion, of imposed eccentricity or conscious underemphasis.

Nor could it have been otherwise. The kind of feudal community in which such figures flourished was already breaking up by the time that Yeats started writing about them. He could still make poetry of them, because their tradition and colour had appealed passionately both to his imagination and his moral sense : but the poetry, had it not been touched by irony, would have had no living reference. Only in the poems addressed to the women he loved, and in the three political poems of the 1916 Rising, did he achieve that simplicity and intensity which create something truly heroic. *A Woman Homer Sung*, *No Second Troy*, *That the Night come*, and those later love poems which

> The poet stubborn with his passion sang us
> When age might well have chilled his blood,

do the same for these women as *Easter 1916*, *Sixteen Dead Men* and *The Rose Tree* do for the leaders of the Easter Rebellion. Though the praise is qualified by thought, the legend remains whole.

It is significant, however, that Yeats should

have been able to write like this about the 1916
Rising, while the Anglo-Irish war produced from
him only verse that was introspective and sometimes querulous.   We seldom get much further
in arguing why one theme has compelled the best
from a poet and a similar one leaves him cold :
but, at the risk of over-simplifying the issue,
I should say that Yeats's special kind of romanticism supplies the answer here.   In spite of, or
perhaps in compensation for, their hard realism,
the Irish have always in their literature taken
more kindly to failure than to success.   The
Easter Rebellion was very much in the tradition
— a masterpiece of heroism and forlorn hope.
Amongst its leaders were several poets and
scholars.   At the same time, and until " the
sixteen men were shot ", it was treated in Dublin
with scepticism and raillery, to some an opportunity for looting, to others the occasion for " a
mocking tale or a gibe To please a companion
Around the fire at the club ".   It was romantic-
ally led and heroically carried through : it had
apparently failed : its tragedy was touched with
glints of the cruellest farce.   It presented, in

fact, the perfect theme for a poet of the Irish aristocratic tradition. But *Easter 1916* is the more magnificent a poem, because the poet never attempts to conceal his initial detachment and incredulity, because he succeeds in the seemingly impossible task of blending realism and romanticism into a heroic whole.

The wars that followed a few years later were a very different proposition. There was little of the romantic about them, and Michael Collins was most untraditionally efficient. Since the whole country was involved, the artist could no longer occupy a ringside seat : he had either to participate or withdraw altogether ; neither enthusiasm nor detachment would work now, and the real gulf between the Anglo-Irish gentry and the Irish common people, bridged for so long by " custom and ceremony ", was finally revealed. To Yeats this seemed the beginning of a period when

> The best lack all conviction, while the worst
> Are full of passionate intensity.

It would be as ridiculous to blame him for his

withdrawal as to have blamed D. H. Lawrence for not being Wilfred Owen. But Spender's criticism that Yeats " found no subject of moral significance in the social life of his time " does hold true here : the development of his verse from 1920 onwards shows that the aristocratic tradition, because the social organisation on which it depended had broken up, now failed — perhaps had failed all along — to give him this " moral subject ".

3

Yeats's connection with the aesthetic movement of the 'nineties at the most impressionable time of his life had a lasting effect. It combined with the inherited aristocratic tradition to offer style, the virtues of courtesy, lucidity and self-possession, as the basis — if not as a substitute — for morality. In *Poetry and Tradition* he wrote, " In life courtesy and self-possession, and in the arts style, are the sensible impressions of the free mind, for both arise out of a deliberate shaping of all things, and from never being swept away, whatever the emotion, into confusion or dulness ". And again, " Three types of men have made all beautiful things. Aristocracies have made beautiful manners, because their place in the world puts them above the fear of life, and the countrymen have made beautiful stories and beliefs, because they have nothing to lose and so do not fear, and the artists have made all the rest, because Providence has filled them with recklessness. All these look backward to a long tradition, for, being without fear, they have held to whatever pleased them."

Pride and independence, courtesy and ceremoniousness — these are the qualities most constantly held up for admiration in his later poems. But they were virtues that played less and less important a part in the changing world about him. Edmund Wilson has written of Yeats, " It may be true that the kind of dignity and distinction which have been characteristic of the poet in the past are becoming more and more impossible in our modern democratic society. . . . The modern poet who would follow this tradition, and who would yet deal with life in any large way, must create for himself a special personality, must maintain a state of mind which shall shut out or remain indifferent to many aspects of the contemporary world."

But it is a tradition too, that, assuming responsibility as it does, prevented Yeats from becoming an "escapist" poet. The various public controversies into which he plunged (though they persuaded him that "neither religion nor politics can of itself create minds with enough receptivity to become wise, or just and generous enough to make a nation"), and his work in the Irish Senate later, are sufficient to show his sense of responsibility. Yet he is, throughout, the aristocratic poet who feels a passionate love for the Cause but also a certain impatience and contempt for the human instruments with which he has to work — a contempt that led him too quickly into disillusionment. Sooner or later, the mood of "the seeming needs of my fool-driven land" always recurred.

Nevertheless, if the nature of his times prevented Yeats from a wider exercise of responsibility ; if indeed he " found no subject of moral significance in the social life of his time "— or, as I should prefer to say, if the moral tradition to which he was born had ceased to be valid ; and if he was thus compelled to fall back upon

> We were the last romantics — chose for theme
> Traditional sanctity and loveliness,

his sense of responsibility towards his art was rendered all the keener. His themes may have been romantic, but he was a realist in his treatment of them : for what is realism in poetry if not the use of the imagination to get beneath the surface of reality and the refusal to put more into the poetry than the imagination warrants ?

Yeats's poetic development was remarkably that of the self-conscious artist. He knew perfectly well what he was about. Even as a young man, with the specious glamour of " popular " poetry enticing him, he was able to turn away and say, " Ireland cannot put from her the habits learned from her old military civilisation and from a church that prays in Latin. Those popular poets have not touched her heart, her poetry when it comes will be distinguished and lonely." In its general reference this comment is academic and a little pretentious : but, for himself, it spoke the true word. He knew what he was doing. He went into politics not least for what they could give to his poetry : and, when he had transferred the blood of nationalism into his own poetic vein, he fell away from politics into the pseudo-philosophical mysticism with which his mind was so curiously streaked. But even now he did not lose his way. By this time he was an old man. Yet, so far from being silenced by age, he turned upon it with the eager ferocity of genius and made it yield up its special riches to him :

> Consume my heart away : sick with desire
> And fastened to a dying animal
> It knows not what it is. . . .

The history of twentieth-century verse shows that, when the moral tradition has failed him, the poet is commonly driven either to prophecy or to nostalgia, or else to a difficult kind of poetry reflecting the isolation of himself and his

friends.   Yeats was not sufficiently naïf to be a
prophetic poet : even his *The Second Coming*, with
its lines

> And what rough beast, its hour come round at last,
> Slouches towards Bethlehem to be born ?

lacks the uncompromising quality, the final un-
reason of prophecy.   Still less, though he wrote
much of the past, can he be called nostalgic : his
later verse is too buoyant, too sinewy for that ; it
is often bitter, but never melancholy in the way
that the verse of the Symbolists is melancholy.

Again, he wrote a great deal about his friends ;
but his tradition compelled him to do so for the
most part with that lucidity which is the artistic
equivalent of good manners : and he wrote a
great deal about himself ; but the tradition,
encouraging a " noble egotism ", enabled him
here to write poems which, though they have no
moral subject to sustain them, are upheld by
sheer strength of personality.   This tradition,
as he understood it, is summed up in the last
two stanzas of *A Prayer for my Daughter*, where
we find virtue represented as a blending of

spiritual anarchism with a kind of temporal good
form :

> Considering that, all hatred driven hence,
> The soul recovers radical innocence
> And learns at last that it is self-delighting,
> Self-appeasing, self-affrighting,
> And that its own sweet will is Heaven's will ;
> She can, though every face should scowl
> And every windy quarter howl
> Or every bellows burst, be happy still.
>
> And may her bridegroom bring her to a house
> Where all's accustomed, ceremonious ;
> For arrogance and hatred are the wares
> Peddled in the thoroughfares.
> How but in custom and in ceremony
> Are innocence and beauty born ?
> Ceremony's a name for the rich horn,
> And custom for the spreading laurel tree.

IX

WILLIAM BUTLER YEATS

BY L. A. G. STRONG

WILLIAM BUTLER YEATS WAS ALL HIS
life a poet. No one in the field of modern
letters so consistently wore the poet's mantle, or
knew so unerringly how to make experience
serve his art. The range of that art, both intellectual and emotional, is wide : yet it was a
distillation. The poet learned to reject all that
might harm it, and to divert to other channels
such of his abilities as did not nourish it. This
knowledge, and this austerity, enabled him to
touch with his poetry rare and common objects,
the solitudes of vision and the things men
squabble over, and to kindle from all a flame of
dignity and passion.

The full art fed on a full life. Wit, student
of magic, shrewd in affairs, a man of inquisitive
and agile mind, he knew both how to manage
his wits and to allow for his genius. Sociable
and a talker, he preserved his poetic personality

from the attrition of casual contacts. His was one of the most formidable minds in Europe ; and no country but Ireland could have produced him.)

Yeats was a difficult man to know, not because he was aloof — this is often said, but it was a misunderstanding, as will appear later — but because he had so many sides and lived on such a high plane of intelligence. He was reserved about his personal life, though he spoke freely of his ideas, and those who had spent hours with him would realise afterwards that, while they had been encouraged to speak of their concerns, Yeats had said nothing about his. So Yeats's *Autobiographies* tell a great deal about his mind, but are incomplete on the emotional side. " Being in love, and in no way lucky in that love " : that is his only account of an experience that provided the finest love poetry in modern English, and, for the very reason that Yeats so ruthlessly made his life serve his art, we cannot read back from the poems to the man. Thus we are unlikely to know more than he tells us.

Those who are interested to investigate what use the poet made of his emotions, and therefore wish to gauge the intensity of the emotions in the man, will find that he has covered his tracks with an old fox's cunning.

At the same time, the *Autobiographies* speak with remarkable candour on the artistic side. Yeats will be fully appreciated only by a mind of calibre equal to his own, but his candour and honesty give chances to the smaller man. From that long tale of acceptances and rejections something may be learned, and the effort at appraisal may rise above impertinence. For, despite the splendour of the poet's mantle, the wearer is what Lady Gregory's pauper would call " a conversible man ". He is not only ready but anxious to establish communication with his reader. The accord must be on Yeats's own terms, but he gives a great deal, and pays the reader the compliment of assuming that he is intelligently interested. He does not try to hide his weaknesses and his follies, and admiration grows as we see how he kept them from weakening his art.

" I am persuaded that at twenty our intellects

contain all the truths we shall ever find." Yeats's all-important early years were stamped with impressions of Sligo and London. Sligo gave the best, for London never won Yeats's affections, and he and his sister lamented fiercely, beside the drinking fountain at Holland Park, their exile from the home of their grandparents, longing for a sod of Sligo turf to hold in their hands.

The boy kept newts in jars, rode a pony — not too well — and liked the ordinary outdoor country things. But he was waiting to grow up. " I remember little of childhood but its pain." " I have grown happier with every year of life as though gradually conquering something in myself." His relatives had character : so had the people he met in Sligo. All were capable of gestures which could nourish a romantic mind. Though his boyhood and youth were to be spent among artists, there was between London and Sligo a difference, paralleled later by the difference between the shapeless sodden faces of certain ragged women seen in London and those gaunter women, crazed with drink, who carried their heads high and strode through the Dublin streets, talking to themselves in loud harsh voices. The Irish people, with their graphic violence of speech, their wild humour and their poetic exaggerations, made magnificent material for him. The cast of his mind was already determined, and the Middletons and the Pollexfens and the country people were stocking it with unforgettable images.

School was difficult for the boy who found it hard to attend to anything less interesting than his thoughts. What he lost there was made up, and more, by his father. John Butler Yeats the painter was a man of vigorous mind, with all his son's love of intensity. He would at breakfast " read passages from the poets, and always from the play or poem at its most passionate moment " to a son who was later to confess : " I only seem to remember things dramatic in themselves or that are somehow associated with unforgettable places ". What a stimulus the father's talk must have been can be gauged from the collections of his letters put out some years ago by the Cuala Press, every one alive with the strength of an authoritative mind. There is much of the father in the son, but the son has strengthened his inheritance : the range of his mind is wider, its muscles more flexible.

From London and the conversation of painters the boy went back frequently to Sligo. Already the struggles were beginning that were to shape his manhood, the search for belief, the effort towards self-possession, the inquiry into the nature of reality. " I did not believe with my intellect that you could be carried away body and soul, but I believed with my emotions, and the belief of the country people made that easy." The conflict between emotion and intellect persists, and what is meant by belief is not solved even in his own later criticisms on *A Vision*. The effort towards self-possession, of which we shall have more to say presently, has yielded not only a manner but a philosophy : and Edmund Wilson, most penetrating of modern critics, said, " Yeats's sense of reality today is inferior to that of no man alive ".

But before going into these questions it is best to finish outlining the life. The young man

studied drawing and painting, listened to Dowden — to whom, when the older man disclaimed
Irish blood, he suggested that Dowden was a
diminutive of O'Dowda : he heard Florence
Farr speak verse, and met Maud Gonne. He
came under the influence of Henley, his first
master. "I . . . began under him my educa-
tion." "I disagreed with him about everything,
but I admired him beyond words." The reasons
must have lain in Henley's character rather than
in his work. The strength of his personality,
its arrogance — Yeats loved arrogance — and its
recurrent suggestion of violence, were all cal-
culated to attract the fiery young man. Above
all, Henley "was quite plainly not upon the
side of our parents". Though his eye was
merciless to personal defects, Yeats was loyal
always to a friend, and his affection for Henley
never weakened. Indeed, when in 1922 he
remarked to me that he had been re-reading
Henley's poems, and added, "I did not think
them very good then, and I do not think them
very good today", there was a note of real sad-
ness in his voice.

Whatever Henley gave, there is no doubt at all about the gifts from Oscar Wilde. Yeats describes the astonishment with which he heard Wilde speak in perfectly finished sentences, and he at once applied himself to learn this art. To the end of his life he would rehearse a sentence or a phrase, saying it over to himself under his breath until it had found the perfect rhythm and cadence.

But that was not the end of Wilde's usefulness. When he remarked that a man could not speak the truth until he wore a mask, he had Yeats's instant and fullest attention. We can only learn the things towards which we have a propensity, and cannot receive knowledge until we are ready for it. Yeats's philosophy of the mask was not a gift from Wilde, but Wilde performed the artist's service of putting into words an idea towards which Yeats's whole nature was striving. Yeats picked up instantly the ideas that suited him, best of all when they were expressed in an epigram, for an epigram offered to him the finished characteristic gesture which he admired above all things, and its " lightning flash " set his passionate imagination ablaze. Wilde's talk was an inspiration, his inexact writing was a warning. He contributed much.

The deepest impress of all, however, was made by William Morris : so deep that Yeats, if he could have chosen to live the life of any man he had known, would have chosen Morris's. Here were poetry, art and politics, each one the expression of a passionate nature : and, even more in tune with Yeats's imagination, here was a man of violent, irascible temper who wrote long romances in which the characters met situations of the utmost embarrassment with an inviolable composure. It would be hard to think of any life which illustrates so strikingly as does Yeats's what A. E. called the law of spiritual gravitation : the law according to which a personality attracts to itself the ideas, the symbols, and the experiences that it needs and is to need.

Yeats was now upon the full tide of idealism ; and he had met Maud Gonne. He mortified the flesh, as in earlier years he had slept in a cave and fed upon buns and tea. Believing that to write in the first person was egotistical, he wrote poems in which the personal emotion (there was plenty of it) " was woven into a general pattern of myth and symbol ". Politically, he found as much to move him, and these emotions too he wove into the pattern. The belief in the golden age, which was merely nostalgic in Moore, led Yeats apart into a world of his own, a world that was less an incitement to action than a haven in which to safeguard sacred things from the rabble. But writing was not enough. He was tireless in the service of Ireland, lecturing up and down the country, spending his personality freely, flinging into the movement all his powers.

The activity taught him a great deal about his countrymen and about himself. The Irishman is difficult to work for. He has a habit of denying patriotism to all who do not think as he does. The bitterness of this discovery, reinforced later on, was to go into many of the poems in *Responsibilities* and elsewhere : but the poet had learned something more important than " Paudeen's spite ". He had learned where his real strength lay, and he had learned the need for a public as distinct from a private personality. "I had sat talking in public bars, had talked late into the night at many men's houses, showing all my convictions to men that were but ready for one, and used conversation to explore and discover among men who looked for authority."

The lesson came pat, to confirm one of the dominant myths of the poet's life. At an early stage of their acquaintance, he had been much excited by a painting of A.E., in which a man standing upon a crag gazed at his shadow flung upon the drifting clouds. Here were expressed Wilde's theory of the mask, and the contradiction between Morris's table manners and the unfailing composure of the figures in his romances. The image of the anti-self had been born in Yeats's mind, an image which was to find constant expression in his poetry and in his life. Everything in those early years converged to drive the lesson home. "In my youth", he was to say, years afterwards, when rallied by A.E. for wearing a top hat at the Horse Show, "I read in that book which I still think the wisest of all books, *Wilhelm Meister* by Goethe, ' The poor are ; the rich are enabled also to seem '. I was then shy and awkward, and I set myself to acquire this technique of seeming. I forced myself to attend functions of every kind until I had it." The technique of seeming, the parrot screeching at its image in the enamelled sea, the birds flying above their shadows in the evening splendour, the manner that, when several people came into the room, changed from intimacy to a performance : all were expression of that dominant myth, which preserved from attrition the greatest poetic personality of our time. Yeats's public manner was in no way insincere. It was a performance in which could be expressed every relevant belief and power, but it was projected.

The meeting with A.E. was important for many reasons. Yeats had always a tendency to visions, and his friend's far greater facility compelled him to scrutinise the whole question. He ceased to accept visions at their face value when the lower half of John Bull presented itself vividly before him : " I could not envisage John Bull as an inhabitant of Eternity ". He decided that such visions were the language rather than the message. They needed interpretation. They were symbols. Once again it is noteworthy how a mind attracts to itself the knowledge necessary to its development. When Yeats fell under the influence of the French symbolists, he was not only ready, but able, to help himself to just as much of their practice as he needed. He had always this mark of the great artist, that he could surrender to an influence, and emerge from it more strongly himself than ever. Blake, Shelley, Ferguson, Douglas Hyde, Standish O'Grady, the French symbolists, Lady Gregory, Synge, Ezra Pound — he found in them all something that belonged to him and helped him to fulfilment.

So, with his natural scepticism sharpened — he had been from childhood balanced between scepticism and belief — he came gladly but with caution to his doctrine of symbols. Symbols meant more to him than to any poet of his age except A. E. They had a fundamental, universal meaning. By their aid the human mind and memory, with its shifting borders, could get in touch with the mind and memory of Nature.

He practised with his uncle, concentrating upon a cabalistic symbol and evoking a scene expressive of its significance in his uncle's mind. Concentrating upon the fire symbol, he set a fellow diner talking of a house on fire. These correspondences, if proved, would add to the magic of his verse. The thought may have been unspoken, but he was by now incapable of doing or thinking anything for which his verse would not ultimately be the gainer.

And so he goes on, developing all sides of his personality, curious, eager, impassioned : pulling himself together for the study of Blake, and emerging with all his convictions deepened — " I had learned from Blake to hate all abstraction " : seeking still for the image cast on the clouds — " I constantly hoped for some gain in self-possession, in rapidity of decision, in capacity for disguise ".

Few poets escape their own mannerisms. Wordsworth did not, Tennyson did not, Swinburne did not. Yeats in his middle years made a complete change and became a better poet.

His progress can be measured by the steps he took to protect his poetic imagination. Tormented from the first by the struggle between the material world and the world of the imagination, a conflict of which the latter so often gets the worst, he had in his early verse avoided the material world altogether, keeping out intellect and " impurities " such as " curiosities about politics, science, history, and religion ". The fairyland with which his early verse was concerned was the equivalent of the sod of Sligo turf he and his sister had longed to hold in London. It was an escape, a symbol of the imagination. There was a sharp division between the real world and that to which the fairy child in *The Land of Heart's Desire* beckoned away the newly married bride. The real world was " too full of weeping " to be understood.

This was a dangerous doctrine, and Yeats saw the danger. The disturbance and disappointment of his love for Maud Gonne was a sharper challenge. He met it partly in terms of his imagined world, among the reeds by the side of the lough, at one remove from the world in which it occurred. Then, when *The Playboy* and all that it stood for rose like a rock in his path, he remembered the advice he had given *The Playboy*'s author ; and the conviction Synge put into his laconic prefaces came at the right time for Synge's preceptor. Yeats put off the embroidered cloak, not only because others had worn it in the world's eye, but for his own sake.

> To write for my own race
> And for the reality. . . .

It was his new resolve, and to achieve it he went back to Ben Bulben and the clear focused images of his boyhood.

> Maybe a twelvemonth since
> Suddenly I began,
> In scorn of this audience,
> Imagining a man,
> And his sun-freckled face
> And grey Connemara cloth,
> Climbing up to a place
> Where stone is dark under froth,
> And the down-turn of his wrist
> When the flies drop in the stream :
> A man who does not exist,
> A man who is but a dream ;

And cried, " Before I am old
I shall have written him one
Poem maybe as cold
And passionate as the dawn."

The new poetry, bare, " withered into truth ",
with its stern architecture of winter boughs,
proved capable of including without loss of
dignity a wider range of subject than any contemporary poet had dared to tackle.   The change
was not only a change of subject, but of rhythm
and syntax.   The old luxuriant rhythms were
gone.

All the heavy days are over ;
Leave the body's coloured pride
Underneath the grass and clover,
With the feet laid side by side

gave place to

Suddenly I saw the cold and rook-delighting heaven . . .

It was an astonishing development, and it
lifted Yeats to the stature of a major poet.   As,
during the succeeding years, his poetry dealt
more and more with the material world, he
continued to put a screen of ideas between that

world and himself. Poetry is not made in the midst of the battle. Yeats decided on what terms to meet the material world, and, with that brilliant intense perception, saw to it that the material world did him no harm. The days of careless spending were at an end. The truth that had now to be spoken, the "terrible beauty", needed a mask. The rebuke which Yeats delivered from the stage of the Abbey Theatre to dissidents on the first night of *The Plough and the Stars* was a very different affair from his speech in defence of *The Playboy*. *The Playboy* speech blazed with the white anger of the man himself : the other was stylised, coming through the lips of William Butler Yeats the dramatist defending a fellow artist from the mob. It was perfectly sincere. The old aristocratic scorn was there, and the old indignation : but they had been passed through a filter. By that time, Yeats had a philosophy which enabled him to face the starkest terrors of experience but also to keep them at a distance : a philosophy nourished by Irish folk-lore, by magic, by theosophy, by Stephen McKenna's translation of Plotinus, by anything which chimed with his thought. His poetry was no longer a refuge from the world. He had crossed to the opposite position, and saved himself for his poetry.

The conflict between contemplation and action took many forms in Yeats's life as well as in his philosophy. In practice it was most often the quarrel in him between the partisan and the philosopher. He was exceedingly effective in the world of affairs, and proud of his cunning. His sense of reality, the shrewdness he possessed in high degree, showed him times out of number how to manage a man or a situation, and the temptation to turn aside was often irresistible. A feeling for mischief aided it. "I must smooth him down", he said softly, when a life-long friend had gone off in a huff. "I must smooth him down." His eyes gleamed behind their glasses, his lips moved silently : and the means adopted, a quite unnecessary display of virtuosity, were brilliantly successful.

This cunning, the knowledge that, if need be, he could beat the knave at his own game, he was obliged as philosopher to disapprove and to disallow. Yeats's difficulty, it cannot be too often stated, was to select from his many abilities those which belonged to him as a poet, and to give the others harmless employment elsewhere. At their best, they established the Abbey Theatre, one of the most remarkable feats of theatrical enterprise in history, calling for shrewdness, business ability, management of things and people, the invention of a special dramatic technique, and the ability to persuade and train the players to make use of it. At their most mischievous, they flourished before a bewildered Censorship official, as an argument against banning Mr. Shaw's *Adventures of the Black Girl*, photographs of sculptures from the Sistine Chapel. The protest had to be made, in the name of art and toleration, but Yeats, who never loved Shaw — how gladly in his *Autobiographies* he records Wilde's epigram, and admits his pleasure at the score off " a notorious hater of romance " — chose with infallible insight a means that would ensure that the ban remained. What could be more persuasive, more suitable, than to show that in that holy of holies, the Vatican, nude statues stood in honour? That as a result Mr. Shaw's book should be indissolubly connected in the official mind with nudity, and the prejudice against it intensified threefold, must be blamed on the official mind, not on the derisive wit that had foreseen and worked for that result.

But there are no flourishes, no mere practical effectiveness, no theatrical gestures in his poetry. "No mind can engender till divided into two." The duality was fruitful.

Another conflict, between scepticism and belief, cut deeper. Yeats had been from the start an intensely religious man, longing always to return to the simple faith of childhood.

. . . Deprived by Huxley and Tyndall, whom I detested, of the simple-minded religion of my childhood, I had made a new religion, almost an infallible church of poetic tradition, of a fardel of stories, and of personages, and of emotions, inseparable from their first expression, passed on from generation to generation by poets and painters with some help from philosophers and theologians.

Later, he tried long and persistently to found a philosophy and a ritual for the imaginary mystical order that was to live in a castle which had taken his fancy. The urge that led him to the Cabala, that was to make him study and reject Plotinus and von Hügel, gave him little peace from boyhood to age. Combining with his need of a philosophy, it is responsible for his studies in magic and his elaborate attempts to formulate the results into a system. Whatever view we take of *A Vision*, it is not hard to account for. We have an almost embarrassing number of explanations. First of all, however, let us take the author's account of how it came to be written. It is based upon automatic writings by Mrs. Yeats, begun very soon after their marriage in 1917. Yeats was at first so excited that he " offered to spend what remained of life explaining and piecing together those scattered sentences ", but received the significant warning that the messages had come to give him " metaphors for poetry ". The messages proceeded to elaborate the distinction between " the perfection that is from a man's combat with himself and that which is from a combat with circumstances ", which Yeats himself had made in what is perhaps his profoundest prose work, *Per Amica Silentia Lunae*. They were accompanied by a number of physical manifestations, and were at times interfered with by interpolations of obvious nonsense. When the study of certain philosophers suggested a revision, further messages came, bidding him let the philosophers alone.

The first thought that occurs here can be put in the words Yeats himself used of Macgregor Mathers : "He . . . thought that when he had proved that an image could act independently of his mind, he had proved also that neither it, nor what it had spoken, had originated there ". The messages were based upon a philosophical distinction of Yeats's own. The supposed sender, when interference was suspected, confessed it, adding — as Yeats puts it —" Had I not divined frustration he would have said nothing ". We can hardly resist asking whether Yeats himself saw that all this might be the dramatisation of something in his own mind ; that it might be his own mind which his wife's subconscious was reading. The creative artist often seems to take down his work from dictation, or to report what he sees and hears, as if he were watching something independent of himself. May not something of the kind have happened here? Did Yeats, in his search for faith, believe what he wanted to believe?

The question is complicated by his attitude towards the finished work. Did he believe it all? He himself answered by another question : " Does the word belief, as they [his questioners] will use it, belong to our age, can I think of the world as there and I here judging it?" And he went on to suggest that the whole might be, after all, a background for his thought, a set of symbols ; " metaphors for poetry ".

This looks like an attempt to have it both ways, to shuffle out of responsibility : but it is not. Holding the view of the material world which he held, he could make no other answer. Yeats believed — and this is no place to go into the evidence for his belief — that images created by the mind could function independently of the creator mind, and assume, if only temporarily, material form. The subjective can walk about the room and leave footprints which will remain visible after it has disappeared. Symbol, or thought, will often call into existence a manifestation associated with it, varying in objectivity with the degree of mediumship available. Such phenomena, if honestly faced, could lead to only one conclusion. The tangible world is a dream, a representation, in terms prescribed by the level and quality of human perceptions, of an eternal reality. Everything in nature is a symbol, in the sense that it is an interpretation put by our senses upon a reality we cannot otherwise know. Belief therefore ceases to be a literal acceptance of the evidence of the senses, or a criticism of experience for apparent failure to conform to that evidence. It becomes an intuition of harmony within a system.

The impatience of many critics for this side of Yeats's work, and their reluctance to face it, seem due to a failure to understand his central position. Believing that all material objects were " representations " or " dramatisations " of a reality which did not end with their destruction, and that their form was decided, more or less arbitrarily, by human perceptions, he naturally drew less distinction than do most men between what everyone sees, which we call reality, and what only a few see, which we call illusion. Suppose, for instance, that of ten people taken to a room in a so-called haunted house, nine felt a vague discomfort, and the tenth saw a toad as big as a calf which jumped at him out of a corner. Most people would distinguish, at least in degree, between the reality of the uncomfortable feeling and that of the toad ; and almost everyone would distinguish between the reality of the toad and that of the furniture in the room. Yeats would, I believe, have made little, if any, distinction. For him, the toad would be a minority verdict : a more vivid representation of a reality equally solid with the rest.

However oddly this may strike the reader, it is at least a consistent theory accounting for all the phenomena within Yeats's range. Mr. Desmond MacCarthy relates an anecdote told him by Edmund Gosse.

" Yeats had told him how he had noticed that a man who was pacing the room was followed by a 'small green elephant'. 'And then,' the poet added, 'I knew he was a very wickud man.'"

Mr. MacCarthy regards this as showing a temporary failure of Yeats's sense of humour. But it, and similar things, were quite real and serious for Yeats. Where most persons would have had an impression of distrust or dislike, the poet's perceptions dramatised the impression into this unusual form. The green elephant was a fact for him, like the man and the carpet on which the man was pacing. The elephant symbolised something in the man : the man symbolised something in eternity. If a man were visited by an angel in his sleep and given a message, the angel would have wings, not because angels have wings in their own world, but because the man would not have recognised it and believed its message if it had not worn the form he associated with an angel. On the great slide-rule of the universe, we focus with our senses only the fraction that lies inside the little glass slide. Some people, and Yeats was one, can move their slide a little, to include as objective phenomena things outside the common focus. Yeats solved the problem by allowing an equal validity to all, and regarding their form as symbolic only.

Towards the end of his life, he inclined a little away from this impartiality, particularly in his poetry, and laid emphasis on the activities of the body. The horror of old age which found expression in so many savage and despairing lines, from

> A sixty-year-old smiling public man

to the description of his soul

> sick at heart
> And fastened to a dying animal . . .

drove him to periods of violent preoccupation with the manifestation rather than that which it manifested. A poet avoids sensuality at his peril : and the passions that, even at their most outspoken moments, were given a Pre-Raphaelite grace in *The Wind among the Reeds*, found an entirely different note. In an early poem, the woman says :

> " O hiding hair and dewy eyes,
>   I am no more with life and death.
>   My heart upon his warm heart lies,
>   My breath is mixed into his breath."

It is a decoration, passion on a tapestry. Later, this is all blown away like mist : she kisses instead, through clenched teeth, crying

> " Strike me if I shriek."

In his final phase, the poet, harking back to the communal simplicities of the ballad, remembered Synge's dictum " All art is a collaboration " : and his last play, *The Herne's Egg*, is a riot of copulation and other men's jokes, lit by flashes of tremendous and erratic poetry.

Several critics have attributed this to the gland operation which he underwent some five or six years before he died. One can imagine his smile at such a superficiality. The life of a man of genius is not so easily charted. The operation did not change his life's current. Instead, we must look to that in him which made him demand the operation : to the manner of man he was.

He said to me once, after he had undergone it, " A.E. should have the operation " and : added swiftly, " He would never consent to it, he would die sooner ".

For Yeats, then, the form of things was a gloss put upon them by the human eye and mind, and he attributed equal value to everything perceived by man's senses at all times. Yet the forms of things were not wholly at the discretion of the perceiver, since there existed the great common mind, the mind of nature, upon which we all could draw, and whose qualities we could evoke by symbols, *i.e.* constant forms. A difficulty arose here, in that some of the evocative symbols did not represent the appropriate quality in the same way as a man's body represents his soul, or a rose-on-earth represents a rose-in-eternity. Instead they corresponded as a word corresponds to the object it designates. But, since for Yeats all symbols sprang from the mind, whether they were representative, an object's

earthly dress ; or evocative, a sort of pass-
word to the mind of nature, it mattered little
in which mind the correspondence was first
established. All symbols, *i.e.* all phenomena,
needed to be interpreted. " The thing heard is
never the message, nor the thing seen the vision."
The lower half of John Bull needed scrutiny
and interpretation, but so did the table, the
chair, the face of a friend. Yeats when I first
met him was passionately interested, with his
wife, in classifying the people whom he met and
in devising a system for their understanding.
(He told me that, first of all, they put me in
the wrong category.) That system he was to
elaborate in *A Vision*, the work of his which has
caused his critics most embarrassment. Edmund
Wilson, for instance, dismisses it as the detritus
of genius, a price we have to pay for the poems.

I said just now that for Yeats belief was less a
matter of scientific evidence than an intuition of
harmony within a system. The question whether
he believed all that was in *A Vision* resolved itself
into the question whether it continued to satisfy
him within its own terms. That he was con-

vinced of its importance to him is sufficiently proved by his revision and reissue of it. In this odd book he clarified and systematised his thought, he arranged and rearranged ideas that nourished his verse : and this at all times was his duty. Yeats knew better than anyone what was good for his genius, when to feast and when to purge. All the questions about the book therefore lead to the same answer. Was it an elaboration of those longed-for beliefs of the countryside, a chart of the fairy world, a system of philosophy for the inhabitants of that castle he imagined in boyhood? Was it a tribute to conscience, an attempt to replace the faith destroyed by Huxley and Tyndall? Was it a code of symbols? Was it an artist's attempt to systematise a background of thought and image which, if not fully understood, might make his poetry vague and chaotic? Was it a full, wise, open-eyed surrender to inspiration, which could, he knew, take many forms? Or was he simply getting off his chest matter which might be bad for his verse?

The clue lies in the reply of the voices, when

in his first excitement he proposed giving up all else and devoting what remained of his life to investigating them : " We have come to give you metaphors for poetry ".

Yeats's interest in magic and the occult needs no separate treatment, being a natural corollary of his belief in symbols and his view of material phenomena as a dramatisation of eternal truth. " The subjective can walk about the room " : it would not have astonished him if you or I had also seen his little green elephant, or if it had left its footprints in sawdust or sand. Magic was but the power of certain symbols to evoke truth in the mind of nature. Ghosts were the form given by our perceptions to the extra-dimensional reality which that form represented.

Yeats was popularly supposed to be learned in magic and to have read deeply in Oriental lore. In fact, he had read very little. He possessed a faculty for instantly seizing and appraising any idea that was going to be useful to him or that accorded with what he knew already : and his magpie treasures were instantly available. With their aid, and his immediate power to see the significance of anything that was said, he could confound scholars, and gained a reputation for immense learning. He had an eagle's eye for what would interest him, and used it, like an eagle, from afar, swooping upon the chosen prey and getting the heart out of it.

He loved abracadabras and sounding names. They added a dignity to life, an impressiveness to speech. They were part of the technique of seeming, the more valuable because the mysteries behind them were real. They were as characteristic of him as the strange curved glasses in which he would offer wine to his friends, and one could believe that he chose his wines as much for their names as for their bouquet, rolling them on his tongue, and ending the recital " and this is Itaalian vairmouth ".

Yeats was a fine example of the unscientific critic, by which is meant the critic who, instead of detaching himself impartially from what he is to inspect, illumines it by surrender to his own prepossessions. No man had a better eye for what was germane to or repugnant from his own thought. Where he was sympathetic, Yeats's criticism is unsurpassed. He had flashes of insight which put him among the masters. But, once off his own lines, he was increasingly uncertain, rejecting whole masses of work which did not interest him, forcing play or poem or novel to his own angle, and exaggerating much for the sake of a little which seemed to chime with his own mind. These prejudices were not conscious. I have heard him utter blistering denunciation of a writer as a man, and a few days later rally in magnificent defence of him as a writer. The work was sacred. A bluebottle, if it could do work which he thought good, would be sure of his advocacy. There was a real nobility in his mind which soared above personal like and dislike. Where he over-praised the work of a friend, it was because he genuinely believed it to be good, not because of the friendship.

Only once did personal feeling sway his judgment. He had for years, and never wholly recovered from it, a blind spot for the works of

George Moore, to whom he long denied any merit at all. Matchless in malice, Moore had thrust at his weak spot as he thrust at everyone's whom he admired. Just as he enraged a virtuous and tolerant choirmaster by saying that he loved not music but choirboys, just as he moved even A.E. to protect himself at law against a projected chapter of *Ave, Salve, Vale* which alleged that he neglected his wife in favour of another lady — both allegations being fantastically baseless — he struck Yeats the unforgivable blow of putting pompous and silly sayings in his mouth : and he was not forgiven.

But these things do not matter. Yeats was not a professional critic. We do not go to him for unbiased judgment, but for the sake of what his bias can tell us. Yeats's thought responding to the stimulus of great work is as revealing as a flash of lightning, and many of the critical *dicta* with which his writings are strewn are of the first order.

The writings which make Yeats's direct contribution to the theatre are the least satisfactory part of his work. His indirect contribution, the work of Synge and the establishment of the Abbey Theatre, would be enough to keep his name honoured in theatrical history. His plays suffer from a vagueness and dimness of characterisation. Admittedly what he was trying to do was alien from the ordinary theatre, where the clash is between character and circumstance. He was bent upon creating a poetic drama, in which the character became a mask, a symbol for the expression of emotion and passionate intensity. His aim was a non-realistic art, the speech of which was poetry. But the aim was not always clearly pursued, the poet's superb sense of character in ordinary life broke in, and, except in some of the later poetic plays, there is an unintended compromise which enables the plays to be compared with other plays, to their dramatic disadvantage.

And, even apart from this compromise, the plays suffer from a positive quality of Yeats's thought. The man to whom symbol and what it represents are almost in the nature of cause and effect, the man, that is to say, for whom the symbol is constant and will always call up its appropriate picture and emotion, will not be at sufficient pains to embody his characters before an audience. The character will already be what he is to represent, before he steps upon the stage. He will be a mask, his face already fixed in the appropriate grimace of mirth or grief. Shakespeare's characters are revealed, not presented. The very quality which is a strength to Yeats's poetry weakened his drama. His plays as a rule read better than they play. There are notable exceptions. *Cathleen ni Houlihan* convinces from the first word to the last, and mounts to a curtain which shook the heart of Ireland and sends a thrill up an audience's spine today. *The Words upon the Window-Pane* is terrifyingly effective either upon the stage or in the study. " When we were reading the play," said an Abbey actor to me, " we said again and again, ' This will never do on the stage '. But when we came to play it, we found he was right every time."

The latest plays, with their freedom from the old compromise, have a power all their own :

yet one cannot resist the conclusion that Yeats was least happy as a dramatist.

His prose is magnificent. Supple in his youth, mannered and stately in his middle period, it achieved a blend of all its old suppleness with an epigrammatic force that was adequate for every purpose. No period, no sentence even, could be the work of another hand, yet it is all natural, and we do not feel, as sometimes in the middle period, that it is the result of labour, and that the order and punctuation are arbitrary. There is nothing against manner and state in writing, but between the hieratic splendours of this middle prose and the ease of the later *Autobiographies* lay the gulf that separated his intimate talk by the fireside from the performance in which he took refuge when people had come into the room and intimacy was impossible.

Yeats's political service to his country was incalculable. Directly he did much, but almost all his real influence came through his work. He gave Ireland a voice when she needed it most.

His theatre — and, when all is said and done, it was his, for the many forces and contributions that joined to make it could have found union under no other personality and no other leader — his theatre and his movement gave coherent utterance to the passions that were being shouted into the air at election meetings.   A national spirit rises like an underground river, finding many outlets : but in the literary and dramatic movement which Yeats led, the purest, the most concentrated stream poured forth and steadily flowed.   Easter week, Eire's present form : how much is owed to " the poet, William Yeats " ? He knew his own responsibility.

> All that I have said and done,
> Now that I am old and ill,
> Turns into a question till
> I lie awake night after night
> And never get the answers right.
> Did that play of mine send out
> Certain men the English shot ?
> Did words of mine put too great strain
> On that woman's reeling brain ?
> Could my spoken words have checked
> That whereby a house lay wrecked ?

It was a popular delusion that Yeats was aloof and incapable of warmth and friendship. The legend gained strength from many witnesses, but it was a legend. True, the poet was not for all comers.

There is not a fool can call me friend . . .

He could magisterially resent a liberty, and the uninvited stranger was soon shown the door. He had no time for bores, or for the self-satisfied and empty. He required of a man that he should have something to say, or else keep his mouth shut. He admired intensely men of action — it must never be forgotten that he knew and loved the country life of the West of Ireland. He was eagerly curious about people, and would, after a brief piercing scrutiny, reach their deepest interest in a few swift questions, and listen, alert as a great bird, to what they had to tell him.

Reverence chilled and irritated him. To approach him as the famous poet was to receive as much of the famous poet's performance as he thought fit to give. But to those who approached him as a human being he was human as any could desire. His best friends in his latter years were young, witty, irreverent men who argued with him, called him W. B., and told him stories. A friendly, sociable man, he felt the legend of his aloofness very keenly : but, unless a person were very tongue-tied, young and unhappy, Yeats lacked the gift for making overtures. Like many a shy man who hides behind a formal manner, he relied on the discernment of his companion. He *could* be aloof, there were many with whom he had no urge to intimacy : but those who say he was incapable of friendship, and of giving brief, surprising signs of the value another human being had for him, merely advertise the fact that they knew him very little.

The mind whom Yeats most resembled was Swift's : the mind whom he most desired to resemble, Blake's. Swift was the subject of his best play and one of his best epigrams : and in the poems, again and again, a terrible phrase recalls Swift's power. The influence of Blake went even deeper. Its centre was in his religious life, whereas Swift's was in daily life and politics.

An aged man is but a paltry thing,
A tattered coat upon a stick, unless
Soul clap its hands and sing, and louder sing
For every tatter in its mortal dress. . . .

Blake, when his brother died, saw his soul carried up to heaven clapping its hands for joy.

But every notice of Yeats must end where it began, with his poetry. Taught by William Morris, Yeats looked on personality as the flame arising from conflict ; and poetry, made " out of the quarrel with ourselves ", was personality expressed in the written word. Many kinds of fuel fed Yeats's flame. It blazed dangerously, it gave off sparks, it sent up smoke, but it was never dimmed. It burned on many levels, and threw strange shadows, illumining a wide circle of life with a fierce realism.

This terrific sense of reality is the basis of all his work. Even at its dreamiest, his poetry was precise in epithet. He insisted always that the poet has to suggest the mystery by tangible means, and is never permitted to shoot beyond them. To open the sluice of imagination as wide as possible, and then to sieve with the most ferocious care what came through it : that was his aim, and he achieved it to a degree unapproached by his contemporaries. However shifting the focus in his philosophy, he would have nothing abstract, loose, or cloudy in his verse. He was the greatest poet of his time because he was the most ruthless, the artist who gave everything to his art. His loves and hates, his speculations, his patriotism, his fears, even the voices from outside, were pressed into service.

The result was a poetry which expressed them all. Yeats's verse gave dignity to everything it touched, from the political idea to the lonely word. He could take a worn adjective and make it live as if for the first time : he could take an idea current in men's gossip and make it a piece of his poem.

The secret was that he never put into his verse anything which his imagination had not fully assimilated. The young Communist poets, whose ideals he respected, he saw fail very often because they filled their verse with lumps of fact and ill-defined abstractions. Yeats never made this mistake. His range was as wide as theirs, and wider : but he knew what they had forgotten, that for the artist it is not enough to know a thing with one's mind. One can do nothing with it as an artist till one knows it with one's imagination. Knowing his own world so, Yeats gave it permanence.

THE END